AQA
Anthology:
love poetry through
the ages

Luke McBratney

Series Editors:
Nicola Onyett and Luke McBratney

HODDER
EDUCATION
AN HACHETTE UK COMPANY

The publisher would like to thank the following for permission to reproduce copyright material:

Acknowledgements:

pp.1, 2, 3: Sir Thomas Wyatt: 'Who so List to Hount, I knowe where is an Hynde' (16th C); **p.5:** from *Shakespeare's Sonnets*, ed. Stephen Booth (Yale University Press, 2000); **p.5: Don Patterson:** from *101 Sonnets* (Faber & Faber, 2012); **pp.7, 8: Andrew Marvell:** from 'To his coy mistress' (17th C); **pp.9, 10: Richard Lovelace:** from 'The Scrutiny' (17th C); **p.11: Marianne Thormahlen:** as quoted in *That Second Bottle: Essays on the Earl of Rochester*, ed. Nicholas Fisher (Manchester University Press, 2000); **pp.14, 15: Lord Byron:** from 'She walks in beauty' (19th C); **pp.18, 19: Christina Rossetti:** from 'Remember' (19th C); **pp.19, 62: Thomas Hardy:** from 'At an Inn' (1898); **pp.22, 23: Ernest Dowson:** from 'Non sum qualis eram bonae sub regno Cynarae' (20th C); **p.23: Carolyn Burdett:** from 'Aestheticism and decadence', © British Library Board, http://www.bl.uk/romantics-and-victorians/articles/aestheticism-and-decadence; **pp.24, 25, 73: Edna St. Vincent Millay:** from 'I, being born a woman and distressed (Sonnet XLI)' from *Collected Poems*, Copyright 1923, 1951, by Edna St. Vincent Millay and Norma Millay Ellis. Reprinted with the permission of The Permissions Company, Inc., on behalf of Holly Peppe, Literary Executor, The Millay Society, www.millay.org.; **pp.25, 26, 27: Robert Frost:** from 'Love and a question' from *Poems by Robert Frost (Centennial Edition): A Boy's Will and North of Boston* (Signet Books, 2001); **p.27: Charlotte Mew:** from 'A quoi bon dire' (1916); **p.27: Michael Schmidt:** from *Lives of the Poets* (Orion, 1998); **pp.28, 29: Louis MacNeice:** from 'Meeting Point' from *Collected Poems* (Faber & Faber, 2013), reprinted by permission of the publisher; **p.29: Edna Longley:** from *Louis MacNeice: A Study* (Faber & Faber, 1988); **p.30: Clive James:** from 'Meeting MacNeice' (Reading For Life, 2006); **pp.31, 68, 86: Keith Douglas:** from 'Vergissmeinnicht'; **p.31: Ted Hughes:** from *Keith Douglas the Complete Poems*, ed. Desmond Graham (OUP, 1990); **pp.32, 33:** from *The Complete Poems of Philip Larkin*, ed. Archie Burnett (Faber & Faber, 2012); **pp.32, 65: Philip Larkin:** from 'Wild Oats' from *The Complete Poems of Philip Larkin* (Faber & Faber, 2014); **pp.33, 59: Philip Larkin:** from 'Talking in Bed' from *The Complete Poems of Philip Larkin* (Faber & Faber, 2014), reprinted by permission of Faber and Faber Ltd; **p.33: Rory Waterman:** *Philip Larkin: Letters to Monica*, as quoted in *Belonging and Estrangement in the Poetry of Philip Larkin*, R. S. Thomas and Charles Causley (Ashgate, 2014); **p.35: Robert Phillips:** from 'Philip Larkin, The Art of Poetry No. 30' from *The Paris Review* (The Paris Review, 1982); **p.36: Elizabeth Jennings:** 'One Flesh' from *The Mind Has Mountains* (Macmillan, 1966); **pp.37, 38: Anne Sexton:** from 'For my lover, returning to his wife' from *Selected Poems of Anne Sexton* (Houghton Mifflin, 2000); **p.40: Seamus Heaney:** from 'Punishment' from *Opened Ground* (Faber & Faber, 2001), reprinted by permission of Faber and Faber Ltd; **pp.40, 41: Edna Longley:** from *Poetry in the Wars* (Bloodaxe, 1996), reprinted by permission of Faber and Faber Ltd; **pp.40, 41: Tony Harrison:** from 'Timer' from *Collected Poems* (Penguin, 2013), reprinted by permission of Faber and Faber Ltd; **pp.43, 44: Paul Muldoon:** from 'Long Finish' from *HAY PB* (Farrar, Straus and Giroux, 1999), from POEMS: 1968–1998. Copyright (c) 2001 by Paul Muldoon. Used by permission of Ferrar, Straus and Giroux, LLC; **p.46: Wendy Cope:** from 'After the lunch' from *Two Cures for Love: Selected Poems 1979–2006* (Faber & Faber, 2009), reprinted by permission of Faber and Faber Ltd; **pp.47, 48, 49: Michael Symmons Roberts:** from 'To John Donne' from *Corpus* (Jonathan Cape, 2004), From *CORPUS* by *Michael Symmons Roberts*, Published by *Jonathan Cape*. Reprinted by permission of The Random House Group Limited; **p.49: Joanna Luft:** from 'Roberts's TO JOHN DONNE and Donne's ELEGY 19' from *The Explicator Volume 68, Issue 2* (Taylor and Francis Online, 2010); **p.50: Carol Ann Duffy:** from 'Carol Ann Duffy b. 1955' (Copyright © 2005–2014 Poetry Archive); **p.60: Pauline Gray:** from 'More about this song' from *BBC* (BBC, 2014), www.bbc.co.uk; **p.60: Northrop Frye:** from *Writings on the Eighteenth and Nineteenth Centuries*, ed. Imre Salusinszky (University of Toronto Press, 2005); **p.64: Robert Burns:** from a letter to Mrs Agnes McLehose (28th December 1787); **p.65: Philip Larkin:** from 'Then and Now, 1993' from *The Times Literary Supplement* (TLS, 12th November 2014); **p.65: J.D. McClatchy:** from *Anne Sexton: The Artist and her Critics* (Indiana University Press, 1978); **p.66: Edna St. Vincent Millay:** 'First Fig' (Poetry, June 1918), reprinted by permission; **p.67: Seamus Heaney:** from 'Feelings into Words' from *Preoccupations* (Faber & Faber, 1984); **p.68: Alexander Pope:** 'A Discourse on Pastoral Poetry (1717)' from *The Works of Alexander Pope, Vol. 1* (John Murray, 1871); **p.72: Robert Burns:** taken from 'Ae fond kiss' (1791); **p.76: Carol Ann Duffy:** from 'The Love Poem' from *Rapture* (Picador, 2006).

Every effort has been made to trace or contact all copyright holders, but if any have been inadvertently overlooked the Publishers will be pleased to make the necessary arrangements at the first opportunity.

Photo credits:

p.3 ©Showtime/Everett/REX Shutterstock; **p.11** © PAINTING / Alamy Stock Photo; **p.18** © Artepics / Alamy Stock Photo; **p.23** Sketch for 'The Outcast', 1851 (oil on canvas), Redgrave, Richard (1804-88) / Private Collection / Photo © Christie's Images / Bridgeman Images; **p.26** © Underwood & Underwood/Corbis; **p.39** © Imagestate Media (John Foxx) / Vibrant Backgrounds SS; **p.41** © Robert Harding Picture Library Ltd / Alamy Stock Photo; **p.47** © PeerPoint / Alamy Stock Photo

Although every effort has been made to ensure that website addresses are correct at time of going to press, Hodder Education cannot be held responsible for the content of any website mentioned. It is sometimes possible to find a relocated web page by typing in the address of the home page for a website in the URL window of your browser.

Orders: please contact Bookpoint Ltd, 130 Milton Park, Abingdon, Oxon OX14 4SB. Telephone: (44) 01235 827720. Fax: (44) 01235 400454. Lines are open 9.00–17.00, Monday to Saturday, with a 24-hour message answering service. Visit our website at www.hoddereducation.co.uk

Impression number	8	7
Year	2020	2019

Cover photo (and throughout) © Anastasy Yarmolovich /123RF.COM

Typeset in 11/13pt Univers LT Std 47 Light Condensed by Integra Software Services Pvt. Ltd., Pondicherry, India

Printed in Dubai

A catalogue record for this title is available from the British Library

ISBN 9781471853838

Contents

Using this guide iv

Introduction vii

1 The poems and poem commentaries 1

Pre-1900 1

Post-1900 24

2 Themes 51

3 The poets' methods 57

4 Contexts 63

5 Working with the text 77

Assessment Objectives and skills 77

Building skills 1: Structuring your writing 79

Building skills 2: Analysing texts in detail 84

Glossary 90

Taking it further 95

Using this guide

Why read this guide?

The purposes of this A-level Literature Guide are to enable you to organise your thoughts and responses to the poems in the *AQA Anthology of love poetry through the ages*, to deepen your understanding and enjoyment of them and to help you to address the assessment requirements in order to obtain the best possible grade.

Note that teachers and examiners are seeking above all else evidence of an *informed personal response to the text*. A guide such as this can help you to understand the text, form your own opinions, and suggest areas to think about, but it cannot replace your own ideas and responses as an informed and autonomous reader.

How to make the most of this guide

We recommend that you adopt the above advice to your individual reading of the poems. The chapter entitled 'The poems and poem commentaries' helps you to consolidate and extend your own knowledge as well as offer you approaches to analysis and interpretation. After you have formulated an individual response to a poem, you might like to read the relevant poem commentary; or you might like to read a larger section or all the poems, unsupported, before reading the relevant pages of this guide.

The subsequent chapters take a broader view and are designed to enable you to see connections across the whole *Anthology*. 'Themes' focuses on how some of the main concerns are explored throughout the poems; 'The poets' methods' considers poetic techniques.

It is vital that you familiarise yourself with the ways your exam board tests your response to the poems. So, use the Specification and the Sample Assessment Materials as your definitive guide to what you need to study and how you are going to be assessed.

Studying the *Anthology* for A-level

Bear in mind the sort of questions you are going to face in the examination. A-level questions are relatively open, and you have a choice between two. Typically, each one invites you to compare how an aspect – for example, a theme or an idea – is treated in two texts. One of the texts is your section from the *Anthology*, the other is your comparative set novel.

Studying the *Anthology* for AS-level

If you are taking the one-year AS qualification, the questions on the *Anthology* invite you to respond to a viewpoint about one of the poems which is reprinted in the examination paper. There are two questions to choose from: one on a poem from the pre-1900 section and one on a poem from the post-1900 section. That means that to be prepared for the exam, you must know every single one of the poems from your section. As part of this it is worth practising responding to different viewpoints on each of the poems. Think of different ways to view each of the poems in class and for yourself as well as making full use of the critical view features throughout this guide.

Key elements

This guide is designed to help you to raise your achievement in your examination response to *AQA Anthology of love poetry through the ages*. It is intended for you to use throughout your AS/A-level English literature course. It will help you when you are studying the poems for the first time and also during your revision.

The following features have been used throughout this guide to help you focus your understanding of the poems:

Context

Context boxes give contextual information that relates directly to particular aspects of the text.

Build critical skills

Broaden your thinking about the text by answering the questions in the **Build critical skills** boxes. These help you to consider your own opinions in order to develop your skills of criticism and analysis.

TASK

Tasks are short and focused. They allow you to engage directly with a particular aspect of the text.

Taking it further ▶

Taking it further boxes suggest and provide further background or illuminating parallels to the text.

CRITICAL VIEW

Critical view boxes highlight a particular critical viewpoint that is relevant to an aspect of the main text. This allows you to develop the higher-level skills needed to come up with your own interpretation of a text.

Introduction

How to approach the poems

A poem is a heightened rhythmic form of language in which ideas and effects are condensed. The best approach is to allow each poem to reveal itself to you gradually. Work in stages: use close reading techniques, participate in class discussions and follow up with your own research.

Initial ideas

Begin with an initial reading: read the title and the poem aloud. If possible, hear it: listen to a recording by the poet or an actor and read it aloud yourself.

After a preliminary reading, jot down some initial notes about the poem's overall meaning, but avoid jumping to conclusions; build your response in stages.

Exploring effects

Build on your preliminary ideas by rereading. Read the poem more slowly. Follow the sense of the poem: when a line is **enjambed** – that is, it does not end with a punctuation mark – carry on fluently to the next. Be guided by punctuation: if there is a full stop, pause and consider what the sentence has expressed. This close, almost line-by-line, approach helps to uncover meaning and allows you to savour poetic effects.

As you reread, consider the methods the poet uses to shape meaning and create effects. Avoid using a checklist of features to seek in every poem. Allow the poem to suggest which features: which ones are of most importance to overall meaning and ideas.

Consider **genre** – whether the poem is, for instance, a **lyric**, a dramatic poem or a narrative poem; whether it is a song, a sonnet or a ballad. When you identify a recognisable genre, explore aspects of that genre through further research. For example, having researched the *carpe diem* genre, you might consider the extent to which a poem like 'To His Coy Mistress' or 'The Flea' is a serious attempt at seduction or a clever piece of verbal dexterity designed to dazzle and impress the poet's peers rather than woo a particular woman.

Consider **form** – the poem's shape and the ways in which it is organised. For example, what are the effects of Harrison using a broken up **Meredithian sonnet** form in 'Timer'? Why is the third quatrain separated into two? What is the impact of the last one beginning with a single line stanza? How does the triplet that forms the final stanza function? (You can find help in answering these questions in Chapter 2.)

Consider **imagery**. How has the poet used figurative language, **personification**, symbolism or descriptive language that summons pictures in the reader's mind?

Again, the amount of attention you pay depends on the poem. 'The Flea', for example, is built around the **conceit** (a striking metaphor that compares two elements that at first seem wildly dissimilar) that the flea is the site in which the couple have already made love and this conceit, and the way in which it develops throughout the poem, deserves close attention. Other poems, however, may not be overly figurative; 'Remember', for example, is a sonnet that proceeds by means of argument and contains little vivid imagery, though a close reading of that argument and attention paid to the more subtle use of images like the speaker being held 'by the hand', or her movement to go then staying, would be revealing.

Consider **aural effects** – that is, effects to do with sound. Poems, such as 'Ae Fond Kiss' and *Vergissmeinnicht* contain strong effects that are relatively easy to identify and comment on. Others, such as 'Punishment' and 'Love and a Question', use rhyme and other aural effects, including **tone** (the tone of voice or mood of the poem, or part of the poem), but do so less obviously.

The big picture

As you consider what you feel are the most important authorial methods, think about the ways in which these methods work together to shape meaning and create effects. After intense work on the detail of selected features you should read the poem a final time to unify it and gain a sense of 'the big picture': what the poem's overall concern is, what it is all about.

Using your comparative novel

If you are following the A-level syllabus, you are going to be studying one section of the *Anthology* alongside a comparative set novel. As you get to know the themes and ideas in this novel, consider how they are similar to and different from those of the poems you are studying. When something in a poem reminds you of something in your novel, note this comparison and think about how you can explore it. Your comparative set novel should give you ideas about your reading of the poems and vice versa.

The poems and poem commentaries

Target your thinking

As you read each summary and commentary, ask yourself the following questions:

- What is your considered personal response to the poem – what do you think are its main concerns? (**AO1**)
- What other interpretations might you offer? (**AO5**)
- Consider the most important methods that the poet uses in the poem: how does the poet use them to shape meaning and create effects? (**AO2**)
- How is the meaning of the poem shaped by your understanding of its contexts? (**AO3**)
- In what ways can you connect the poem's themes, ideas or methods to other poems in the *Anthology*, or to your comparative novel? (**AO4**)

Love poetry through the ages (pre-1900)

Sir Thomas Wyatt (1503–42), 'Who so list to hount'

The speaker tells whoever wants to hunt that he knows the whereabouts of a deer. While his hunt has been unsuccessful, he is compelled to continue. Changing tack, he advises that anyone who hunts this deer wastes his time and he describes the deer's collar: 'in diamond letters there is written "Don't touch me, for I belong to Caesar, and while I look tame, I am wild to hold"'.

Commentary Wyatt is credited as bringing the **sonnet** form from Italy to England, and 'Who so list to hount' is often considered a reworking of Petrarch's 'Rima 190' – a sonnet that presents a lovelorn speaker chasing a white doe which is freed and disappears at the end of the poem. He retains the two-part structure of a Petrarchan sonnet: a group of eight lines (an **octave**) is followed by a group of six (a **sestet**). But note how Wyatt adapts the sestet, making it conclude with a **couplet** – a feature typical of later sonnets in English including those of Shakespeare.

He also departs from Petrarch in his exploration and structuring of the poem's subject matter. In a Petrarchan sonnet, the **octave** commonly presents a situation or problem, which the sestet responds to or solves. In Wyatt's sonnet, the normal structure is reversed: the *consequences* of a situation (an unattainable love) are presented (in the octave) first, then the sestet describes the situation that led to those consequences.

Throughout, Wyatt presents the speaker's vacillating feelings and evokes a **paradoxical** desire that both draws and defeats. The first line – 'Who so list to hount, I knowe where is an hynde' – seems a hearty exhortation to other men to join his hunt (for deer or, metaphorically, for women); yet the next line offers a contrast – he feels unable to continue to hunt. The second line marks this change of mood with the contrastive conjunction 'But'; it goes on to give prominence to the speaker's lovelorn feelings by placing the sighing onomatopoeic word, 'helas,' in the middle of the line, with both a preceding and a following **caesura**. Such a sense of world-weariness persists until the fourth line when the speaker acknowledges that he is 'of them that furthest cometh behinde'. The fifth line, however, marks a shift in mood with another contrastive conjunction –'yet' – as the speaker's attention shifts back to what draws him to the deer.

This sense of vacillation is also aided by the form. For example, the first four lines (or **quatrain**) make an **envelope rhyme**. There are two rhymes: the one made by the first and the fourth lines and the one made by the first and the second. This enclosing of the middle lines makes them stand out and draws attention to the suffering caused by desire: 'But as for me, helas, I may no more/ The vayne travaill hath weried me so sore'.

The speaker's feelings are also suggested by **aural effects**. As the octave progresses, 'f' sounds accumulate to different effects: first, in combination with short vowel sounds they suggest the quick bounds of the deer 'as she fleeth afore'; secondly, they emphasise the fruitlessness of pursuit: 'Faynting I followe. I leve of, therefore'. Note how this line disrupts the light iambic meter with a **trochee** at the beginning of the line – 'FAYNTing' – which uses a faltering beat thereafter, underscoring the speaker's faltering, then abandoned, attempt to follow his desire. The octave concludes with a metaphor of futility: 'in a nett I seke to hold the wynde'. The hunter is ill-equipped for his task, his actions are foolish and his quarry so elusive as to be both intangible and invisible. Petrarchan sonnets contain a **volta** (Latin for 'turn'): a change in the direction of the argument, or a shift in the mood at the beginning of the sestet. Here, the first half line of the sestet repeats the first half of the poem's first line with a subtle change: it is 'who list *her* hount', not 'who so list *to* hount' (my emphasis). We have closed in on the specific prey, and the poem retains its sense of vacillation as we both think of the poem's opening and anticipate its ending. Wyatt's methods change subtly too as, after line ten, instead of revealing the feelings of the speaker, he offers the reader **imagery** associated with the deer. We move from the wide angles of the octave – which included glimpses of the fleeing deer – to focus on her more directly, moving close enough to see her neck and then the writing on her collar.

The inscription on the collar is prominent – and not just because its words conclude the poem. As noted above, rather than follow the usual rhyme scheme of a Petrarchan sonnet in the sestet, Wyatt concludes with a couplet, whose words stand out as a new voice in the poem – words which resonate in the reader's mind: '*Noli me tangere*, for Cesar's I ame/And wylde for to hold, though

I seme tame.' They command anyone who comes this close not to touch, as the deer is defined as the property of a powerful man.

While offering a conclusion, the couplet is also consistent with the vacillating quality that has been pronounced throughout by ending on a paradox. The hart embodies a contrast between seeming and being: while she seems tame, she is actually wild. We might ponder the significance of 'wylde to hold': as well as suggesting the hart's untameable nature, could it imply her owner's power to punish anyone who dares touch her; or might it suggest her promise of wild sex?

'Who so list to hount I know where is an hynde' therefore, explores feelings surrounding obsession or unattainable love. As well as the presentation of the speaker, you might like to consider the deer. Is she simply an object, pursued by one man and possessed by another? Or might the poem be said to give her a voice — albeit one that emerges only through the writing on her collar which marks her as someone's property?

Context

Sir Thomas Wyatt was a courtier and one of King Henry VIII's intimates during the time when he was arranging Henry's marriage to Anne Boleyn. Later, when Anne was being tried for adultery, Thomas was imprisoned. While Wyatt was released, many claim that he and Anne were lovers. 'Who so list to hount' is often cited as evidence for this, with the poem being read as an **allegory** in which the speaker represents Wyatt; the hind, Anne Boleyn; and Caesar, Henry VIII.

Context

Experience dramatisations of the intrigue between Wyatt and Anne Boleyn by reading *Wolf Hall* by Hilary Mantel (2009) or by watching the BBC television adaptation directed by Peter Kominsky (2015).

Taking it further ▶

Borrow some history books, or conduct some internet searches to find out more about Anne Boleyn's character and her potential relationship with Wyatt. In what ways might such historical understanding inform your reading of the poem? For example, you might compare the presentation of the hind in the poem to some accounts of Anne's attractiveness and of the alleged behaviour which resulted in her trial and execution.

◀ Several accounts suggest that, while not classically beautiful, Anne Boleyn was an alluring woman, with a powerful sexual magnetism. This still from *The Tudors* shows Anne (Natalie Dormer) and Henry VIII (Jonathan Rhys Meyers)

William Shakespeare (1564–1616), 'Sonnet 116'

In Ang Lee's film version of *Sense and Sensibility* (whose screenplay was written by Emma Thompson, who also plays the role of the sensible Elinor) 'Sonnet 116' is used. When the ill-matched Willoughby and Marianne recite it to each other, Willoughby gets the words wrong.

Shakespeare's sonnet explores the qualities of ideal love, stressing its enduring nature. Real love doesn't change when circumstances change; it is a constant, like a star that guides a ship. It is not subject to time and lasts until doomsday.

Commentary The poem is an **English** (or **Shakespearean**) **sonnet**, comprised of three **quatrains** and a **couplet**; it is part of a sequence of 154 sonnets written by Shakespeare in the 1590s. The first 12 lines are framed by allusions to the marriage ceremony: the clergyman invites the congregation to 'declare any impediment' that might prevent the marriage and he then asks the couple to promise to love each other 'till death us do part' and to confirm the legality of their marriage as they 'will answer at the dreadful day of judgement when all secrets shall be disclosed'. Such allusions lend a solemnity to the subject of love, and indeed the poem remains a popular secular reading at weddings today.

Each quatrain offers comment on the nature of love in a confident declaratory tone. The first concludes with the declaration that love isn't true love if it wavers according to changing circumstances. The abstract language means that the reader can supply the details: alteration might, for example, refer to a change such as the illness of a partner, a loss of status or fortune or even an infidelity. Note the paradoxical quality of the statements and the repetition of parts of the same words in 'love is not love', 'alters when it alteration findes' and 'bends with the remover to remove'.

While the nature of love's challenges remains undefined in the second quatrain, Shakespeare's imagery grows more concrete as a range of metaphors from seafaring characterise love as life's guiding light. Love is compared to an 'ever fixed marke' – that is, a flaming navigation beacon – and the Pole star by which mariners navigate – the 'star to every wandring' ship. To take the height of a star was to measure its altitude to be able to steer by it; this idea is alluded to in 'whose worths unknowne, although his higth be taken'. Like a star whose true worth is unknowable, love is a mysterious force.

The final quatrain shifts to characterise love in even more grandiose terms: as being unchangeable in the face of time. Love and time are personified, with Love being presented as 'not Times foole'. While the lovers are subject to the normal physical changes that time brings – losing the youthful good looks of 'rosie lips and cheeks' – real love remains constant and endures 'even to the edge of doome' (the end of time).

There is a shift in mood as, in the couplet, the poet reflects on what he has written: this serves to emphasise the strength of his convictions, though some may feel it superfluous and that it adds little other than a boastful challenge to the reader.

To what extent does Shakespeare's language delight and make the reader appreciate his message about love's constancy? Or might such clever language – in keeping with the couplet – suggest the self-conscious wit of a poet who enjoys showing off his skills?

Context

Sonnets are usually associated with love. Yet by the time Shakespeare was writing his, the form was also used as a way to order thoughts about other topics, such as time and death. Indeed the structure of the English sonnet - three quatrains and a couplet - suits developing an argument of two premises (statements) and a conclusion. Furthermore, by Elizabethan times sonnet writing had become a way for the poet to prove his poetic prowess as much as a way to win a lady. As Don Patterson argues 'The exploits of the Elizabethan sonneteers ... have more than a whiff of testosterone-fuelled competition about them' (Patterson, 2012).

Taking it further ▶

Find out more about early modern ideas of the 'marriage of true minds', and compare Shakespeare's presentation of this notion and the concept of being parted, yet remaining together to those presented by his contemporary, John Donne, in 'A Valediction: Forbidding Mourning'. In this poem, Donne compares two lovers who are about to part to the twin legs of a pair of compasses – a comparison that he develops ingeniously throughout the poem.

TASK

How might you compare the ideas of love in 'Sonnet 116' to ideas of love in the novel you are studying. For example, if your novel is *The Great Gatsby*, to what extent is Gatsby's love for Daisy presented as similar to the true love that Shakespeare writes about? (Include comment on some of the details towards the end of Chapter 6 of *The Great Gatsby* in your comparison.)

John Donne (1572–1631), 'The Flea'

The speaker's loved one has refused him sex. He asks her to consider a flea, which has bitten them both. This flea, he reasons, shows how insignificant her refusal is – after all, their bodily fluids have mixed inside it without shame or loss. The flea – where they have had sex – is a holy place which he begs her not to destroy. She kills the flea; but, after questioning her killing of this innocent creature, he claims that its death proves how false her fears of sex with him are – doing so would cause her no more harm than did the death of the flea.

Commentary The poem is a typical Donne love **lyric** and also a *carpe diem* poem: one in which the speaker invites the **addressee** to seize the day – that is, to make the most of the present (often by accepting his sexual advances).

CRITICAL VIEW

One editor, Stephen Booth, makes the following comment about Sonnet 116: 'The more one thinks about this grand, noble, absolute, convincing and moving gesture, the less there appears to be to it' (Booth (ed.), 1980). To what extent is this a fair assessment?

Context

Discover more about the references to seafaring and astrology and the figure of the fool by visiting: www.shakespeares-sonnets.com/sonnet/116

This website also offers interesting readings of 'Sonnet 116' in its context within the sonnet sequence and as a love poem written to a man rather than a woman.

5

Using the **conceit** of a flea to represent the sanctity of the couple's relationship and embody their physical union before it has actually taken place, the poem is set up as a witty and unusual way to talk a woman into bed. Note the speaker's tactics. For example, he first uses the flea as a symbol of the holiness of their union; then he suggests that it is the place in which their union resides; and, in a new line of argument, that the flea's death – which causes the addressee no harm – provides evidence to show that she will suffer no harm or loss of honour when she yields.

The poem's form helps to develop its argument. Each elaborate stanza is comprised of a **sestet** (of three couplets) and a **triplet** (three lines with the same rhyme). In the sestet the speaker develops the point clearly, using each couplet as a building block in that argument: note how the first line of each couplet is often **enjambed** or has only a comma for punctuation, while the second ends with a more definite pause indicated by punctuation such as a full stop, question mark or a colon. At the beginning of the triplet, there is a shift in the argument, as the speaker extrapolates from what the sestet has proved. For example, arguing, in the first stanza, that the flea, gorged on their blood has done more than them, or, in the second, that the addressee should spare the flea's life. That each line of the final three rhymes adds a subtle persuasiveness as this harmony and subtle shift in tone helps to emphasise the speaker's point, which is also reinforced by the final two lines being longer than the others – two lines of **iambic pentameter** in a poem that is largely written in **iambic tetrameter**.

Biblical language also lends weight to the argument. What the modern reader might think of as a disgusting creature is elevated by terms like 'marriage temple' and 'cloistered'; there are also echoes of the Christian Trinity in the idea that the flea is three persons: both the man, the woman and itself.

TASK

Consider your response to the speaker. Do you admire his cleverness and think of this as a romantic poem which speaks of a strong love? Or do you find him insistent – even aggressive – casting aside the woman's objections and denying her any real voice? Might the poem be seen as an exercise in style, as the poet takes on a fashionable topic, the mock encomium (a poem that celebrates a person, event or idea)?

Taking it further ▶

Find and listen to the podcast on 'The Metaphysical Poets' from Melvyn Bragg's Radio 4 series, *In Our Time*. What do you learn about the features of metaphysical poems and the concerns of the metaphysical poets?

Context

In early modern times, fleas were much more common in homes than today and it is likely that contemporary readers would not have been revolted by the poem's flea imagery in the way that some modern readers are. The idea of the flea sucking the blood of both lovers would have slightly different connotations to Donne's contemporary readers since they believed that sperm and other sexual secretions were formed by the body's purest drops of blood and thus that blood mingled during sex.

Andrew Marvell (1621–78), 'To His Coy Mistress'

The speaker says to his apparently shy or modest loved one that, if there were sufficient time, he would spend thousands of years praising her beauty; but their time is limited and they must make the most of it and enjoy physical love while she is young and he is full of desire.

Commentary The poem shows the influence of Donne and the earlier **metaphysicals** in its subject matter and methods. Witty and persuasive, it is an example of a *carpe diem* poem, and, like 'The Flea', it uses the force of logic to persuade the woman to have sex. It follows the structure of a syllogism – a logical argument in three parts: two premises (statements, or propositions) and a conclusion.

The first premise states how long the speaker would spend wooing the addressee. Note how the durations grow as the **verse paragraph** progresses. For example, he would spend 'An hundred years ... to praise' her eyes and gaze at her forehead, but 'Two hundred to adore each Breast' and 'thirty thousand to the rest'. The speaker's tone is ambiguous: is this a sincere praising of a mistress, or is there something humorous – even mocking – about what he says? These lines are reminiscent of the **blazon** – the poetic tradition of cataloguing the woman's attractive features, often moving down her body as the poet does so. Perhaps Marvell mocks the typical exaggeration of the blazon by providing such an exaggerated example: far from being a love-struck and courtly appreciation, Marvell's blazon seems lecherous: he spends half as much time on the eyes and forehead as he does on each breast and three hundred times as much on the regions that lie beneath.

The pace picks up in the second premise, which is almost half the size of the first and states that their time is limited. The **personification** of time as a charioteer, with one hand on the chariot and the other holding a scythe is a common image from Greek mythology, but look how Marvell makes it work. There is a subjective sense of actually hearing time's approach: hearing it 'alwaies' and hearing it 'hurrying near'. It is vivid, immediate and frightening. Unlike other accounts of love, there is no sense that it will endure beyond the grave; there is no mention of any Christian afterlife: all that awaits the dead lovers are 'Desarts of vast Eternity'.

The later images are macabre. In her grave the addressee won't hear her lover, and graveworms will take her virginity. The imagery of worms contrasts with the earlier playful use of phallic imagery in which the speaker's love was described as 'vegetable' – that is, taking a long time to grow, which some read as being suggestive of a long slow erection. Perhaps this section is designed to shock the addressee into acceding to the speaker's wishes. It goes on to echo the funeral service from the Book of Common Prayer: the speaker describes his lust turning 'into ashes' and the addressee's 'Honour' to 'dust'. It ends with humour that mocks her coyness with an epigrammatic flourish: 'The Grave's a fine and private place/But none I think do there embrace'.

Taking it further ▶

In one of the manuscripts of the poem in the Bodleian Library the last four lines of this verse paragraph (from 'And your quaint' to 'do there embrace') are omitted. To what extent do you feel this shorter version alters the poem's meaning, and how might it affect your response to the speaker?

TASK

Some editors believe that in the final verse paragraph the last word of the first line of the word should be 'glew'. They argue that this word, which is found in two manuscripts from two separate sources, is what Marvell intended – not 'hue'. Meaning sweat, and having sexual connotations in this context, 'glew' has secondary meanings of glow and of perfume. If you were editing the poem which word would you include, and for what reasons?

CRITICAL VIEW

While the poem can be read as a humorous academic exercise that plays with notions of the *carpe diem* poem and takes them far beyond its limits, it can also be read less ironically and from a feminist perspective. For example, you might wonder, why it is always the male who is the one luring or pressurising the female into a sexual liaison.

The speaker spells out his conclusion as the final verse paragraph develops:

> Now let us sport us while we may;
> And now, like am'rous birds of prey,
> Rather at once our Time devour,
> Than languish in his slow-chapt pow'r.

Note the cluster of words drawn from a **semantic field** of time: the 'now's and the 'at once' give a sense of urgency. Action seems much more attractive than the passivity of wasting away through the slow eating of time. **Aural effects** also suggest the contrast: compare the short vowel sounds of, for example, the 'am'rous birds of prey' to the long vowels and drawn out 'l' sounds of 'languish in his slow-chapt pow'r.'

The poem lacks spirituality; instead it glories in physicality. Note how, for example, the poem gives a visceral feeling of the coming of Time, a sense of the decomposition that will come with death and – towards the end – how it exhorts the couple to behave like wild, dangerous animals in their love-making. Far from the slow tenderness of some love poetry, there is great vigour – even violence – in Marvell's depiction of sex: the couple should 'devour' time, 'tear [their] Pleasures with rough strife'. There is a strong sense of mutuality and momentum as they 'ro**ll** a**ll** [their] Strength, and **all**/[their] sweetness up into one Ba**ll**'. Note the ways in which Marvell uses sound – through such effects as internal rhyme and repetition – to echo this sense; the ball is also an image of motion and two having become one.

After the image of the wrecking ball of love that bursts through 'the Iron gates of Life', the pace slows and Marvell adds a final thought: 'Thus, though we cannot make our Sun/Stand still, yet we will make him run'. Reminiscent of Donne's 'The Sun Rising', Marvell's speaker articulates the conceit that the couple, mere human beings, control the sun. Their love making will affect their perceptions so that the sun and the whole world will change.

Context

This **trope** (of a male speaker seducing a female addressee) seems not to be confined to centuries' old poems; think, for example, about the sexually suggestive lyrics of Marvin Gaye's seminal soul song 'Let's Get it On' (1973). An internet search should reveal the song's suggestive lyrics and help you find out more.

Taking it further ▶

Consider the more recent intertextual use of the famous soul song in 'Marvin Gaye' by Charlie Puth, featuring Meghan Trainor (2015). Unlike 'Let's Get it On' and the *carpe diem* poems in the *Anthology*, this pop song is a duet that gives space to both male and female voices. When Puth and Trainor both sing 'Let's Marvin Gaye and get it on' it seems that this is not a seduction involving a dominant and a passive partner, here the sexual feelings and the desire to act on them are mutual.

Richard Lovelace (1618–57), 'The Scrutiny'

It is morning and the speaker and his lover are mid argument. She has questioned him about his promise of monogamy, but he explains that keeping such a vow is impossible. He must seek out new women. If, after he has done so and still finds her agreeable, he will return to her and their relationship will be better than ever.

Commentary Even the very title – 'The Scrutiny' – displays the speaker's attitude towards love. He looks coldly and weighs up both the addressee and his options. We begin in medias res (in the middle of the action) with the speaker attacking the addressee verbally over a promise that he supposedly made. His haughty tone and quibbling language – 'why should you swear I am foresworn' – start the poem in a selfish and arrogant manner. The word 'Lady' at the start of the third line is a trochee: its stress on the first syllable draws attention; it is followed by a caesura, and it might be pronounced ironically – can she be a lady if she's jeopardised her reputation by sleeping with a rake such as him? Thus, cruelly, the addressee is distanced verbally as the speaker tries to extricate himself from her physically.

Typically, lovers perceive time as moving fast when they are together and slowly when they are apart. In 'The Scrutiny' it seems that the speaker can't escape quickly enough. The cluster of temporal references seem more than selfish; they sound insulting: he speaks of his love being 'much and long,/ A tedious twelve hours' space'. What is more, since the poem seems to be the speaker's words to his lover after they have woken up together; he is more or less admitting that he has used her for sex.

The reduction of women to hair colours is like the sexist way in which some men used to refer to women: objectifying them through terms such as blondes, brunettes and red heads. There is even an argument that the hair he refers to is of a more coarse and sexual kind. The metaphor of the mineralist, who searches for treasure underground, might support this idea. It elevates the man and denigrates the woman: his promiscuity is raised to the level of an art, since dowsing (being a 'mineralist') requires rare skill and intuition. Like earlier love poems, such as Donne's 'To his Mistress Going to Bed', in which the speaker exclaims: 'O my America! My new found land', the man is the active explorer and the woman the passive land or the 'treasure' waiting to be discovered.

A modern reader is likely to find the speaker's attitude in the final stanza sexist, even though his tone seems more gentle. He offers the possibility of returning to the addressee after he has gorged himself on sex with other women – is 'sated with variety' – and compliments her looks by calling all the other women 'meaner beauties'. Note how the stanza opens with a conditional clause – 'Then, if when I have loved my round,/ Thou provest the pleasant she' – suggesting that the speaker might return to the addressee, but that she needs to be meek and compliant. In addition, his comments about his sexual adventures are self-aggrandizing: like a victor from battle, he has been 'crowned' and won 'spoils' – though his exploits have left him battle weary, with terms like 'sated' and 'spent' perhaps suggesting sexual exhaustion. Indeed, rather than choosing to return to the addressee and her virtue, the speaker could be so worn out by his adventures that he may need to use her again – this time more for comfort than sex.

An alternative reading is possible if we consider genre. In Lovelace's time, poem was set to music, performed and received as a song; it was not intended to be read and studied. Even today, songs use clichéd situations and extreme emotions to make them appealing, and people often pay more attention to their tune and the evocation of drama and emotion than their words. 'The Scrutiny' is certainly dramatic and immediate. The familiar dramatic types of the rake and the wronged woman are used as is the familiar situation of a break up, and the poem creates immediacy through aspects such as its frequent use of the present tense and passionate speech. It is easy to imagine this song appealing to its original listeners, who, it might be argued, were not so attuned to its gender politics as we are today.

The Tribuna of the ▶
Uffizi by Johan Zoffany:
Like travelling after
university or taking a gap
year, the Grand Tour could
be both a cultural and
sexual experience

CRITICAL VIEW

'The Scrutiny' is
little more than a
misogynistic fantasy
that privileges
male desire and
objectifies women.
How far is this view
consistent with
your reading of the
poem?

Taking it further ▶▶

Why not compare 'The Scrutiny' with some more recent love poems that dramatise break ups? For example, you might like to consider one or more of the following by Owen Sheers: 'Keyways', 'Valentine', 'Winter Swans' or 'Four Movements in the Scale of Two'.

Rochester (1647–80), 'A Song (Absent from thee)'

The speaker explains that when he parts from his love he will weaken. While facing torment in the world, he is compelled to go. When tired of adventuring he will return to the bosom of his love. If he strays from her again and has another worthless sexual encounter he may die unforgiven and damned.

Commentary The poem is a song and articulates the feelings of an unfaithful man, exploring aspects of the compulsion that makes him stray from his true love despite knowing this causes nothing but pain. The pain is twofold: being separated from his true love and being tormented as a result of his debauchery.

From the outset, desires for infidelity are presented as compulsive. Like one in the grip of an addiction, the speaker is compelled to act on them even though they will lead to trouble. He knows he will 'languish'; he knows he is a 'straying Fool'; but he is helpless to do anything else.

The second stanza begins with a passionate exclamation and a conclusion arising from what he said in the first: '*Dear*, from thine Arms then let me flie'. The earlier sense of his straying as being irrational is continued when he calls his mind 'Fantastick'. In this case the word means given to fancies, or capricious. Unlike Lovelace, who presents philandering as a mysterious art like dowsing for precious stones, for Rochester it has tortuous consequences. 'Torments' will be the results of his speaker's infidelities and they will 'tear [his] fixt Heart from [his] Love'.

The first line of the penultimate stanza is slowed and given a sad sound by the alliterated 'w's of 'When wearied with a world of Woe' and there is a marked contrast between the miseries of infidelity and the comforts of faithfulness. The virtues of 'Love and Peace and Truth' are said to flow from her 'safe Bosom', where he could 'expire' contentedly. This either means he could, at last, breathe easily there, or that he could happily die in her arms; 'expire' also has connotations of sexual climax.

After this romantic image of the wanderer reunited with his true love, the speaker returns to the fears of infidelity. 'Lest' means 'in order not to' or 'in case'; the final stanza opens with this word and shows the alternative life that the speaker will lead if he fails to return to his true love. If he wanders from this 'Heav'n', he is likely to 'fall on some base heart unblest'. As well as conveying a sense of sin, the phrase might suggest the dangers of sexually transmitted infection. Note the sense of self-loathing in the following line with its accumulation of harsh 'f' sounds as he almost curses himself at the thought of being 'Faithless to thee, False, unforgiv'n'. The consequences of such a fall are clear: he will lose his 'Everlasting rest' – that is, lose the contentment of being with his true love and the peace of an afterlife in heaven.

CRITICAL VIEW

Consider the view that 'the relationship between the speaker and his addressee resembles the one between an errant sinner and God' (Marianne Thormählen in Fisher (ed.), 2000). In what ways do you find this view convincing?

Build critical skills

Review the poems which are in the form of songs. What common features can you discover?

Thus the poem is touchingly ambiguous: the reader feels the affection in which he holds the addressee and understands that the speaker realises the stupidity of infidelity – and the mental torture and ultimate damnation that it brings. We suspect, however, that the attempt to return to his true love will fail; the words 'once more' in the first line of the final stanza suggest that he knows his own patterns of behaviour and is unlikely to change.

William Blake (1757–1827), 'The Garden of Love'

The speaker recounts an experience of returning to a green where he used to play as a boy. It has changed: a chapel has been built; the area is covered in graves, not flowers. Above the door of the chapel is the inscription: 'Thou shalt not', and black-gowned priests are on patrol, painfully holding him back from his pleasures and desires.

Commentary Blake was an individualistic thinker, who feared the corrupting influences of institutions, such as the monarchy, the government and the Established Church. While a committed Christian, he was a dissenter – that is, he worshipped outside of the constraints of the Church. The poem can be read as an **allegory** for the ways in which the Established Church of the eighteenth century (the Church of England) controls people's actions, thoughts and even their love and desires. Note how the Church has corrupted the **pastoral** idyll: what was once a beautiful open green space, full of 'sweet flowers' and associated with love and 'play' now contains 'graves' and 'tomb-stones' and is a place where desires are forbidden and joys are constrained.

If we look more closely, we can see how the poem works. The first quatrain sets up a story told using simple bi- and **monosyllabic** words. The metre and rhyme contribute to the simplicity: Blake uses a bouncing iambic tetrameter and a simple abcb rhyme. But look how this pattern is disrupted when the evils of the Established Church intrude: an extra syllable emerges at the end of the first line of the second quatrain – 'And the gates of this chapel were **shut**'– and the words '**Thou shalt not**' contain harsh stresses and stand out in this prominent position at the centre of the poem. Thus, the reader is given a sense of things being forbidden. It is noteworthy that we don't discover what exactly we should not do; it seems that anything and everything we desire is denied.

At the final quatrain the transformation is complete. We have moved from the **Pastoral** genre to the **Gothic**: once green space is now grey and black; gardens have become graveyards and joy has been replaced by pain. Note how sound reinforces meaning as internal rhymes cluster in the final two lines mimicking the binding that takes place deep within the speaker as the

> Priests with black **gowns** were walking their **rounds**
> And binding with **briars** my joys and **desires**.

Context

You may be familiar with his 'Jerusalem', which is part of the preface to Blake's long poem *Milton* and was set to music by Sir Hubert Parry in 1916 and has become, to many, a rousing alternative national anthem. Some read the 'dark satanic mills' as being symbolic of industrialsim, others as symbolic of the Established Church.

Like a perversion of Christ's crown of thorns, the final image is one of pain and humiliation, but such feelings have been internalised and are for no higher purpose. By analogy, those subject to the Church's harsh rule are controlled not just externally (as by the Priests who patrol in the penultimate line) but internally through having been made to accept its teachings and the modes of thought they engender. As in another of Blake's poems, 'London', 'The Garden of Love' depicts people being held tightly in the grip of 'mind forged manacles' – that is, controlled by their oppressors from within.

Robert Burns (1759–96), 'Song (Ae fond kiss)'

The speaker asks for one kiss from his loved one, before they part for ever – a parting which will bring him much sadness. In this situation, he feels his best hope is leaving him and he is surrounded by despair. He describes the intense love he feels for her and reasons that the pain of his broken heart would have been lessened had he loved her less intensely. He bids her farewell and wishes her every happiness for the future.

Commentary Burns' poem is a sincere expression of powerful feelings of love. In the eighteenth century, sentiment was one of the most pervasive literary styles and this poem is written in that mode: it privileges feelings over intellect and it offers sincerity rather than irony or wit. Burns' use of different emotions associated with love helps to keep the poem from seeming cloying or repetitive: there is a subtle balancing of feelings of deep love and deep pain as he thinks about the imminent parting, which he makes seem even more emotive by using the dramatic verb 'sever'. In addition, the poem is written as a song (in which heartfelt emotion is commonplace); in this genre, a detailed outpouring of love is appropriate, rather than seeming to be overstated.

Everything about the poem serves to intensify the expression of powerful loving feelings. There is no complex stanzaic pattern or rhyme scheme; rather, Burns chooses simple quatrains that are rhymed aabb. The metre puts a stress on the first syllable of every line, but ends each line with an unstressed syllable. Lines that end in this way are known as **feminine endings,** and in this case they lend the poem a sad, falling rhythm, which is also aided by the use of **feminine rhyme** (rhymes made by unstressed syllables). A simple vocabulary, mostly of monosyllables – which in the first two quatrains is drawn primarily from a semantic field of sadness – also helps to give the start of the poem a gloomy mood.

The first stanza voices the depth of the speaker's love by expressing how he is 'deep' in tears, which are 'heart-wrung'. Note the sounds that contribute to the stanza's rich effects: onomatopoeic 'sighs' and 'groans' are used as well as three-part rhymes – 'I'll pledge thee' and 'I'll wage thee' – which proclaim his ongoing affection for and allegiance to his loved one. In the second stanza the despair reaches its nadir (low point) and is evoked through imagery of darkness and light: the speaker's loved one is 'the star of hope' that has gone, leaving him with no 'cheerful twinkle' and only 'dark despair'.

Build critical skills

How do hidden pressures or constraints prevent love, or lead to suffering, in the novel you are studying? For example, if you are studying *Tess of the D'Urbervilles* compare how Hardy uses the religious graffiti in Chapter 12 with Blake's use of the chapel and the inscription in 'The Garden of Love'.

Context

Considered the national bard of Scotland, Burns is a much-loved poet. After Queen Victoria and Christopher Columbus, there are more statues of Burns in the world than any other non-religious figure. Many people meet on Burns Night (25 January) to mark his birthday, for a supper that includes readings, haggis and whisky.

Taking it further ▶

Access the BBC website devoted to the life and search for the work of Robert Burns, where you can find both readings of 'Ae Fond Kiss' as well as relevant biographical material.

Thoughts of his loved one, however, lift the mood from gloom to something closer to celebration. Note the cluster of uses of the words 'love' and 'lov'd' at the end of the third and the start of the fourth stanzas. This is the very heart of the poem, and at the very heart of the poem is love.

The speaker's final thoughts are for his loved one's well-being; he wishes her 'ilka [every] joy and treasure,/Peace Enjoyment, Love and Pleasure!' and then the poem returns to the thoughts of the first stanza. While the first and the last stanzas look identical, there is a subtle difference: the second line of the first reads 'Ae fareweel **and then** for ever!', but the second of the last reads 'Ae fareweel, **Alas**, for ever!'; while there is a cyclical effect of nothing having changed, the time for parting has moved closer and 'Alas' adds an additional sense of emotion by denoting another sigh.

Build critical skills

How is your appreciation of 'Ae Fond Kiss' shaped by knowing more about Burns' biography?

Context

The song was written for Agnes 'Nancy' McLehose, a cultivated lady who was separated from her husband who was working in the West Indies. Burns was deeply in love with her and they corresponded daily in 1787 and 1788. It is thought that their relationship was unconsummated, though her maid bore Burns a son in November 1788.

When, in December 1791, Burns heard that Nancy was travelling to the West Indies to see her husband, who hoped for a reconciliation, he sent her a copy of 'Ae Fond Kiss'.

Lord Byron (1788–1824), 'She Walks in Beauty'

A beautiful woman is described as being like a cloudless, starry night. She encapsulates a sense of harmony and beneath her fine face lie serene thoughts. Her expressions are not only pleasing, but they suggest goodness and purity.

Commentary This lyric expresses the wonder, admiration and awe occasioned by being in the presence of beauty. For centuries, beauty has been associated with harmony and symmetry – even today psychologists argue that those with symmetrical features are perceived as being attractive. Symmetry and harmony are notable elements within the poem. 'She walks in beauty, like the night/Of cloudless climes and starry skies' compares the living breathing, walking woman to a night of beautiful contrasts – one that is dark and cloudless, yet illuminated by many stars. Notice how Byron balances those elements of dark and light. For example, in the third line he uses 'cloudless climes' to set off the 'starry skies'; and in the fourth the 'dark' is used to balance the 'bright'.

Balance is also mimicked by the use of literary features. You probably noticed the alliteration which links 'cloudless climes' and which helps them to contrast with the 'starry skies', but notice too the way in which the end rhyme at lines

1 and 3 helps to set off the contrast between 'night' and 'bright'. The poem's formal regularity is also noteworthy. The rhymes are completely regular throughout and a steady iambic tetrameter creates a regular up and down rhythm. Only once does it vary: in line 4 of the first stanza, which begins with a stressed syllable on 'meet':

> And **all** that's **best** of **dark** and **bright**
> **Meet** in her **asp**ect **and** her **eyes**:

While this draws attention to the beauty of the woman in which the best of opposites meet, it also allows the regularity to seem even more marked through the variation.

There is something of the **blazon** tradition in the poem as Byron catalogues the beauties of her 'cheek', 'brow' and 'smiles', yet Byron's final thoughts are not for features of the body, but of the heart. It seems that the woman's outward beauty is the result of inner goodness and purity. Her beautiful features 'tell of days in goodness spent'; she has no guilty conscience – her 'mind [is] at peace' – and the love she feels is either chaste or she is not in love at all.

The woman then is idealised spiritually as much as physically. This sense is also conveyed by the use of religious language in the poem's first two stanzas. Take the first line – the idea of walking in beauty is unusual, but it might remind us of the idea of walking in the light of God (see, for example, Isaiah 2:5), and the sense of heaven denying such tender light to the 'gaudy day' might suggest that heaven is allowing the beauty of this woman to appear in the night. Indeed the idea of 'nameless grace', while primarily connoting elegance, might also remind us of the Christian concept of grace, which is being granted forgiveness by God. Certainly the final stanza, which culminates in an exclamation about the woman's goodness, peace and innocence, makes her sound more than beautiful, more than graceful – almost saintly.

Context

A friend of Byron, Sir James Webster-Wedderburn, wrote that Byron was inspired to write the poem the day after meeting a beautiful woman called Mrs Wilmot at a party in London.

It is said that, on the night of the meeting, Mrs Wilmot was in mourning and wore a black dress with glittering silver sequins.

John Keats (1795–1821), 'La Belle Dame sans Merci.' A Ballad

The speaker sees a sickly-looking knight and asks him what the matter is. The knight recounts the story of how he met and fell in love with a beautiful woman who was half human and half fairy. After a day of love, the beautiful woman sang him to sleep and the knight had a terrible dream: he saw pale kings and princes who told him that 'La Belle Dame sans Merci' had him in her power. When he woke he was cold and alone on the side of a hill. That, he tells the speaker, is why he looks unwell and wanders aimlessly.

Commentary As the subtitle states, the poem is a ballad – a poetic retelling of a folk tale about a tragic incident rendered in vivid manner and usually in quatrains whose second and fourth lines rhyme. Keats' ballad is set in medieval times and uses direct speech to explore the experience of a knight who saw a lady, who turned out to be much more than met the eye.

The first three quatrains establish the setting. It is autumn – a season of transition between summer and winter, which is appropriate for a tale of transition from euphoria to despair. Details like 'the harvest's done' and 'no birds sing' might be read symbolically and as foreshadowing the gloomy events to come. The lily is a symbol of death on the knight's forehead as well as his literal colour in consequence of his fever and anguish.

At first glance, stanzas IV to VIII and the first line of stanza IX seem to depict an idyllic love, as the knight meets the beautiful woman, adorns her with flowers, places her on his horse and then she in turn gives him food, shelter and kisses. But, look closer and you can see supernatural and sexual subtexts. The woman's long hair might suggest sensuality; her light foot, quick and unpredictable behaviour. The quality of her eyes is given impact by 'wild' being placed at the end of the description, **end-stopped** and as the last word of the stanza. It has connotations of her elfish unpredictability, but also might also suggest the promise of wild sex. Some feel that the 'fragrant zone' not only denotes a belt made of flowers, but also connotes female genitals, and the conclusion of the stanza, where she makes 'sweet moan', might support such a reading. In addition, the way 'she looked at [the knight] as she did love' suggests sexual confidence, and the long hours she spent on the knight's 'pacing steed' might be a metaphor for a long session of sex.

After three stanzas that begin by focusing on the knight's actions, the next two and the first line of stanza IX focus on the actions of the woman, which grow progressively more supernatural. The foods that she feeds the knight seem to be from another world, and the language that she speaks is paradoxically 'strange' yet intelligible. When the knight is taken to her 'elfin grot', the woman behaves strangely: she cries and sighs sorely. We are not given the reason for this mood swing, and it remains a mystery after the knight kisses her 'wild wild eyes' twice each, she then lulls him to sleep, which brings on a terrifying nightmare.

The nightmare is recounted in stanzas X and XI. The pallor of the men in the dream recalls the pallor of the knight himself in the early part of the poem and it seems that the fate of these people is that of the knight. Note the close-up descriptions of these past victims, the last one being an image of their lips gaping wide as they form a 'horrid warning'.

The poem closes with a cyclical effect as the words, while from the knight's and not the speaker's perspective, are almost identical to those of the first. Thus, the reader is given a sense of the knight's entrapment: there will be no progression from his sorry state; he, like the 'pale kings, and princes', is condemned to a loitering life of discontent.

While the poem might seem to be a fashionable piece of mock medieval balladry, Keats might be using this genre to explore the nature of obsession or addiction. The 'Kubla Khan' **allusion** (see the **Context** feature) might make us think of being under the influence of drugs and how after extreme highs it can be difficult to deal with normal life. Love might be the main intoxicant explored: having experienced extreme love, it might be difficult to return to normal life without it. Certainly the idea of sex with one who is immortal might suggest such a reading, but also there could be the idea of the crushing depression that can come from being abandoned by one who was loved intensely.

Context

Manna is a bread-like substance that God gave Moses and the Israelites to eat when they were in the desert; 'honey wild' might remind us of food in the 'land flowing with milk and honey' which God promised to Moses. See Exodus 16.18 and Exodus 33.3 of the *King James Bible*. A further **allusion** might be to Coleridge's famous dream poem, 'Kubla Khan', which concludes: 'For he on honey-dew hath fed,/And drunk the milk of paradise'.

◀ To what extent do you feel that this painting by John William Waterhouse (1893) captures aspects of Keats' narrative accurately?

Christina Rossetti (1830–94), 'Remember'

The speaker expresses her thoughts and feelings about how she would like the addressee to think about her when she is dead. She is unwell and addressing her loved one, whom she would like to remember her. In the last six lines the speaker's mood shifts: she expresses the idea that she would rather the loved one forget her than become saddened by memories of her.

Commentary This Petrarchan sonnet explores issues such as love, death, memory and control within relationships. The first eight lines – the octave – seem insistent that the speaker be remembered. Including the title the word 'remember' is used four times; indeed, the first word of each quatrain (we can divide this octave into two distinct units of four lines each) is a verb in the imperative mood, commanding the addressee to 'Remember'. The situation seems touching: the speaker is in love with the addressee and she would like their relationship to endure beyond death through his remembrance of her; the sense of a life ended before its natural span is also moving – we have the image of the couple hand-in-hand and the idea that their planned future is not to come to pass. In addition, the melancholy mood is compounded by the poem's strong sense of religious belief. Yet rather than offering happiness, the afterlife is presented as the 'silent land' – a refuge from the 'darkness and corruption' of the world.

The **stanzaic form** contributes to the poem's meaning. Each of the quatrains that comprise the sonnet's octave uses **envelope rhyme**. The first is rhymed abba, which gives the central rhyming lines increased prominence, and the fourth line rhymes with the first, adding a sense of looking back rather than forwards. The central lines present a gloomy vision of the afterlife in which the couple are separated – when the speaker is 'Gone far away into the silent land;/ When you can no more hold me by the hand'. The second quatrain offers a sense of time running out. Once death comes there will be no more daily planning of the couple's future; it will be too late for thoughts of cures, palliatives or divine intervention ('to counsel then or pray').

language

There is a marked **volta** at line 9: the poem turns to develop a completely different line of thought. The **internal rhyme** on 'yet' and 'forget' draws further attention to this shift as the speaker introduces a new mood of uncertainty: if the addressee should forget her for a while he should not grieve, because, if there remains a hint of the 'thoughts that once' the speaker had, he should forget her and be happy, rather than 'remember and be sad.'

At first glance, this seems a loving and considerate thought: many readers feel that, above all, the poem expresses an optimistic and altruistic wish for her lover's wellbeing after her death. Yet something more complex might be going on. Why, for example, is life represented by darkness, and what are the thoughts that the speaker once had, which, if remembered in part, mean that the addressee should forget the speaker?

Indeed, if we return to the poem with such doubts in mind, we might consider an alternative reading. In the following lines, note how the addressee is the subject of the sentence and the speaker the object: 'When you can no more hold me by the hand'; 'You tell me of our future that you planned'. Might the speaker be constrained by the addressee, who makes her decisions – plans her life for her? Read in this way, the poem might be read as one in which a woman is trying to break free from the control of a man.

Thomas Hardy (1840–1928), 'At an Inn'

The poem narrates the experience of the speaker and the addressee going to an inn. While they were not lovers, those working at the inn assumed that they were. The speaker considers the reasons why love did not come to them and the poem concludes with the speaker reflecting on their present situation of desiring to be together, but being separated by distance and marriage to other partners.

Commentary 'At an Inn' is a reflection on love that might have been. Narrated in the first person plural, the speaker speaks for both himself and his female companion. There is black humour at work as those in the inn speculate about the couple and take a vicarious enjoyment in their assumed sexual relationship: they 'warmed' as they supposed the couple 'more than friends' and wished to God that '… bliss like theirs/Would flush [their] day!' The direct speech conveys the excited, gossipy pleasure that the onlookers feel, but, ironically, their conclusions are wrong.

Despite exciting sympathy in others, love is not what the couple experience: 'never the love-light shone/Between us there!' After two stanzas of warm and active language, the poem turns cold and static: breath is 'chilled' and a buzzing fly is 'palsied unto death'. The kiss that those at the inn expected 'Came not' and 'Love lingered numb'. It is as though a cruel joke has been played as the couple are rendered insignificant by this **personification** who toys with them for his 'sport'. Note the contrasts between the descriptions of imagined love and the couple's real experience. The language of the former is free-flowing, easy – clichéd even – as the onlookers feel sympathy 'With living love/Which quicks the world'; alliteration, **parallelism** and a fast even pace make such emotions almost too easy to experience. Yet the **caesura** and the 'maybe' at the end of the line hint that real life is not so straightforward.

The following lines are the climax – or rather anti-climax – of the story. Comment on the poetic techniques that Hardy uses to make this a memorable and effective part of the story.

> Yet never the love-light shone
> Between us there!
> But that which chilled the breath
> Of afternoon,
> And palsied unto death
> The pane-fly's tune.

TASK

Analyse Hardy's use of narrative in the poem. Comment on how it is structured, how it uses time and the significance of its location. Think about the perspective from which it is narrated; comment on the inclusion or absence of the woman in the story.

(In this context, we can take 'But' to mean only or instead.) The final stanza has moved far from the comical tone of the first as it draws serious conclusions from the story. Much older, the speaker reflects on the differences between appearances and reality. While years before the couple looked in love but weren't, now they don't seem to be, but ache with love for each other. The speaker's tone becomes more passionate: note the use of **apostrophes** and a sentence that is grammatically an imperative but punctuated as an **exclamatory**. He **apostrophises** to the 'severing sea and land' and the 'laws of men', imploring them that he and the **addressee** be allowed to stand together as they once did that day at the inn.

Context

The poem was inspired by Hardy's relationship with the aristocratic and literary Florence Henniker. Their growing friendship and her congeniality, polished manners and lively interest in Hardy led him to draw the wrong conclusions about their relationship. Having persuaded her to visit Winchester Cathedral with him, Hardy took her to *The George*. Despite those at this inn thinking them lovers, Florence drew the line at flirtation; her Christian beliefs meant that Hardy would never be more than a friend.

Taking it further ▶

Consider the poem as an example of the 'the one who got away'. Think, for example, of people who look up former boyfriends or girlfriends on social media long after they have split up.

Taking it further ▶

Florence Henniker inspired one of Hardy's most memorable female characters, Sue Bridehead, in his final novel, *Jude the Obscure* (1895). You can find out more about this novel and about Florence in Claire Tomalin's biography: *Thomas Hardy: The Time-Torn Man*, London: Penguin, 2006.

Thomas Hardy (1840–1928), 'The Ruined Maid'

POEM SUMMARY

The poem dramatises a chance meeting in town between two women originally from the same village. The one still living in the country is impressed by the other's clothing and asks where she got such finery. 'O didn't you know I'd been ruined' she replies. The poem continues in this pattern as the countrywoman asks about jewellery and adornments, polished speech, smooth hands and a lively personality. The answer is the same: such things have been gained in consequence of her having been ruined. The countrywoman wishes for the things her friend has, but she is told she can't expect them: after all, she isn't ruined.

Commentary Hardy offers a comic take on the idea of 'the fallen woman' – the term given to one who had sex without being married. For a Victorian woman, this usually meant ruination: one who had an illegitimate child, for example, would often be shunned and could end up impoverished or fall into prostitution.

It is unclear whether the **eponymous** character is a prostitute or the mistress of a wealthy man, but Hardy uses her wealth and sophistication to **satirise** the idea that a woman is ruined by pre-marital sex. As you can see from several of the poems in the *Anthology*, men have been at liberty to pursue their sexual desires without any sense of them being ruined. Indeed the term 'ruined' functions like a running joke in the poem, with the idea that a woman can be ruined becoming progressively more ridiculous.

(margin handwriting: CONTEXT + MESSAGE OF POEM.)

The poem entertains through comedy. Its long lines bounce along with a predictable beat, and the construction of each quatrain – with three lines for the countrywoman followed by a line of comic reply from her friend – establishes a pattern that means the reader knows when to expect a punchline. Note also the comic contrasts between the speech of the two characters and how Hardy uses tone, accent and dialect. Look at the third **quatrain**, for example: the countrywoman draws attention to her friend's former use of archaic pronouns like 'thee' and 'thou' and expressions like 'thik oon' and 'theäs oon', before exclaiming that 'Your talking quite fits 'ee for high compa-ny!'; after this the ruined maid replies with poise, fluency and concision that 'Some polish is gained with one's ruin'.

The final stanza concludes the poem with the countrywoman wishing for the clothes, the poise and the looks that her counterpart has, but is denied them as, in the words of her friend, 'You ain't ruined'. It is interesting to consider how the ruined maid's speech comes closer to that of the countrywoman at this point: we can imagine the sophisticated woman about town as the simple field worker that she once was.

(margin handwriting: ALTERNATE VIEWPOINT.)

Although primarily to amuse and entertain, the poem may also be read as a direct and satirical attack on the treatment of working-class women in Victorian England, who it seems have only two options: to be exploited through hard agricultural work, or to be exploited for sex.

Taking it further ▶

Compare how Hardy presents the idea of the fallen woman in the poem with the ways in which he treats the same subject in *Tess of the D'Urbervilles*. After having sex with Alec, Tess might be considered a fallen woman. Think, for example, about the ways in which she conceals her past and the consequences of this concealment.

◀ Richard Redgrave, *The Outcast* (1851). A daughter, who has given birth to an illegitimate child, is being expelled from the family home by her father

21

Context

Ideas and phrasing from Dowson's poem are used by the character Lois Lane in the song 'Always True To You (In My Fashion)' from Cole Porter's 1948 hit musical *Kiss Me Kate*. An internet search on YouTube should allow you to hear the song.

Compare the song and the poem, considering mood, situation and other areas you feel are important.

Build critical skills

The title of the poem comes from the *Odes* of the Roman poet Horace and translates as 'I am not as I was in the reign of good Cynara.' Consider the effects of Dowson using such a Latin title. Similarly, why do you think he uses the name Cynara for the lost love?

Ernest Dowson (1867–1900), *'Non sum qualis eram bonae sub regno Cynarae'*

The speaker remembers with passion the previous night when, while kissing another woman, he was besieged by thoughts of a former love – a woman called Cynara, whom he declares he has been faithful to in his own way. He describes the feeling of being physically close with the woman – whom we infer was a prostitute – while preoccupied with yearnings for Cynara. His riotous behaviour is recounted, but even amongst wild dancing he was pining for Cynara. Despite asking for wilder music and more potent wine, his yearning thoughts of Cynara render his nights joyless. As he has done at the end of every stanza, he declares that he has been faithful to Cynara 'in [his] fashion'.

Commentary This rich and emotional poem expresses an obsession with a lost love. Caught up in the intensity of the first person narrative, the reader is swept along by the speaker's feelings and given a sense of his debauched lifestyle through fragmentary details such as a 'kisses', a 'warm heart'; 'roses', 'music' and 'wine'. It is unclear whether the loss of Cynara came as a consequence of riotous living, or if losing her led to him adopting this way of life.

The language is both **rhetorical** and **archaic**. Everything seems heightened. The poem does not attempt to be realistic: in presenting a powerful obsession for a former love, it offers more than realism and seems more interested in evoking mood and feelings than telling a realistic story in a realistic way. The **archaic** diction – using terms like 'betwixt' and 'yesternight' as well as inverted syntax such as 'there fell thy shadow' – helps to give the poem a sense of gravitas as do the regular alexandrines (12-syllable lines in **iambic hexameter**) which allow the speaker to linger on the emotion of every line. This is a poem of excess which rarely does something just once. For example, the first line says both 'Last night' and 'yesternight' and the experience of the memory of Cynara is evoked twice: first as a 'shadow' that falls between his lips and those of the prostitute, then as her 'breath' which was 'shed/Upon [his] soul'. Furthermore, the speaker explains how he was 'desolate and sick of an old passion', then repeats this sense of desolation in the next line and adds that he 'was desolate and bowed [his] head'.

Perhaps the most memorable literary feature of the poem is one of repetition: refrain. 'I have been faithful to thee, Cynara! In my fashion' is a wonderfully ambiguous statement – simultaneously proclaiming fidelity while suggesting infidelity. You might like to think about the extent to which this is an honest declaration, or an unpleasant excuse. Note how the forceful **exclamatory sentence** with which each stanza reaches a climax is undermined by the final anticlimactic three words. Another refrain is also used in the fourth line of each stanza, though, unlike the last line, this one varies subtly as the poem progresses. Note how 'And I was desolate and sick of an old passion' in the first stanza becomes 'And I *am* desolate and sick of an old passion' (my emphasis).

While the idea of being faithful in his fashion remains constant, his sickness and desolation only grows worse – to the point where it is no longer a memory of the past, but a present condition.

STRUCTURE

The poem's regularity also adds to its impact. The rhyme and metre bring a sense of familiarity to the reader as he or she is carried along in the wave of emotion. Each stanza is a **sestet** comprised of two **tercets**, each of which uses **envelope rhyme**. This rhyme scheme has the effect of drawing attention to the middle line; this is particularly the case with the fifth line of each stanza, which also draws the reader's attention as it is shorter – a line of **iambic pentameter** (ten syllables comprised of iambs) rather than an alexandrine. For example, the reader is drawn to the feeling evoked by the penultimate line, and the idea of the speaker being 'hungry for the lips of [his] desire' lingers long after the final refrain has been read.

FORM

While it is, of course, important to consider the poem's themes, meanings and the ways in which its literary features create effects, don't neglect the sheer enjoyment and entertainment value that it brings. Features like regularity, rhyme and refrain are associated with oral poetry. While you have much to learn about it through analysis, you may have just as much to gain through performance: so don't just read and think – recite it aloud!

Context

Dowson is associated with the Decadent Movement of the late 1890s. While decadence literally means falling into a state of decay, in relation to literature of the 1890s it refers to several interlinked qualities, which include:

the notion of intense refinement; the valuing of artificiality over nature; a position of ennui or boredom rather than of moral earnestness or the valuing of hard work; an interest in perversity and paradox, and in transgressive modes of sexuality.

(Carolyn Burdett, 'Aestheticism and Decadence')

Love poetry through the ages (post-1900)

Edna St Vincent Millay (1892–1950), 'I, being born a woman' (1923)

After a night of passionate but casual sex, the speaker explains how her natural female instincts made her body respond to his; this rebellion of feelings over intellect led to her yielding. Despite this, she won't remember him lovingly – in fact, when they meet again she may not even speak.

Commentary The poem is a **Petrarchan sonnet**. The octave offers an explanation of the speaker's instinctive feelings that led to the addressee winning her sexually. The sestet begins with a clear **volta** – a shift in mood – as the speaker turns more directly to the **addressee** and tells him how she will think about him and how she will behave towards him when they next meet.

Note how the sonnet portrays the influence of both the head and the heart and plays with the reader's preconceptions about female psychology. It begins by ironically living up to masculine notions of women being fragile, needy and in thrall to their emotions: because the speaker is female she is '**distressed**' by 'all the **needs** and **notions** of [her] kind'. The diction is decorous and ladylike – Millay talks of the addressee's appearance as 'your person' and refers to him being near using the old-fashioned noun 'propinquity'. Then the language takes a sensual turn as she dramatises female lust in a vivid image of feeling 'a certain zest/To bear your body's weight upon my breast'. This shift is witty and comical; 'zest' makes the sexual act sound exciting and enjoyable, but the subtext of the next line is perhaps more serious. The alliterated 'b's link the idea of '**b**ear[ing]' and the lover's '**b**ody's' weight on her **b**reast', lend it a heaviness, or sense of discomfort. To 'bear' carries connotations of endurance or suffering and might also remind us of childbearing – for women, sex can lead to the suffering and pain of labour. Rather than a frivolous commentary on women and their whimsical feelings, therefore, the octave might point to sexual inequalities; its last three lines come after a colon and express general ideas that arise from the speaker's particular experience. This is just how things are: it's the way 'the fume of life' is designed; sexual feelings override the intellect and lead to women giving themselves to men.

While the octave might, on one level, show female weakness, the sestet shows female strength; here the speaker's strength grows as thoughts of emotions give way to the speaker's controlling intellect. The earlier sexual feelings are dismissed as the 'treason/Of my stout blood against my staggering brain'. It is as if a mutiny took place within the speaker, which overpowered her and left her rightful ruler – the brain – temporarily wounded. Yet the speaker's voice grows increasingly confident, and much more idiomatic and conversational than the more mannered language with which the poem began.

Build critical skills

Compare the presentation of female sexuality in this poem to that presented through a character in a comparative novel such as *The Awakening*. For example, how do the levels of frankness and sexual freedom compare in the texts? How much is the character in control of her sexuality in comparison to Millay's speaker?

Context

While Modernist writers were experimenting with new forms and difficult allusive, Millay satirised such writing, she invented a mocking maxim: 'straightforwardness is wrong, evasion right'.

At the sonnet's close, the brain is fully in the ascendancy as the speaker cleverly manages to sound almost polite while being both witty and insulting. For the addressee, love is out of the question. The speaker won't even pity him; the only emotion left is scorn – a strong feeling of contempt or mockery. In case the addressee is in any doubt, she spells out her feelings in the last two lines. While not technically a couplet, they have the air of finality that we often find at the end of a Shakespearean sonnet; the speaker declares:

> I find this frenzy insufficient reason
> For conversation when we meet again.

Having spent the night with her, the addressee might have had the chauvinistic impression that he would be able to do so again, but Millay's speaker makes it clear that she regards their physical coupling as no more than a kind of temporary insanity – a 'frenzy' – and that, in future, the addressee is unlikely to have even social intercourse with her.

▲ Popular, critically-aclaimed and rich, Edna St Vincent Millay (1892–1950) was one of the most rebellious and liberal voices of the 1920s

Robert Frost (1874–1963), 'Love and a Question' (1913)

A stranger comes to the door of a house in which a bridegroom and bride are honeymooning. He asks the groom for shelter. The groom stands on the porch and asks the stranger to look at the sky with him – presumably, to check if the weather is going to be too harsh to spend the night outdoors. Inside, the wife longs for her husband. The groom looks at the road but thinks of his bride. The stranger is given money, bread and a prayer. The poem ends on a question: should the groom spoil the love between himself and his wife by sheltering the stranger? He does not know the answer.

Commentary This deceptively simple narrative poem leaves its main character impaled on the horns of a dilemma: should he leave his wife on his honeymoon night to extend hospitality to a needy stranger; or, more broadly, should romantic love have precedence over brotherly love?

The first stanza generates sympathy for the stranger:

> He bore a green-white stick in his hand,
> And for all burden, care.
> He asked with the eyes more than the lips
> For shelter for the night
> And he turned and looked at the road afar
> Without a window light.

He is characterised by naturalistic descriptions, unlike the groom or the bride: the only external description of the groom is the adjective 'fair'; the bride is later described in terms of her face being 'red rose' with the glowing of the open fire and the even more symbolic imagery of her heart in the third stanza. The tramp or beggar figure's awkwardness at having to ask for help is rendered by his looks and the way in which he turns to the dark open road, perhaps allowing the bridegroom to appreciate the grim alternative to hospitality. Note also Frost's subtle use of **zeugma** (pronounced **zewg**-ma, this term denotes one verb qualifying two nouns in different senses): the man 'bore' both a 'green-white stick' and 'care'. This suggests that the man's troubles are as obvious as the stick he carries, which resembles either a walking stick or a weapon (there is, after all, something discomforting about being in a remote place and answering the door to a stranger at night time).

The bridegroom does not invite the stranger inside, but does not send him away either: he chooses the middle ground of going out to the porch with him, foreshadowing the conclusion of the poem where the question of the title – whether love should be jeopardised by admitting sorrow into the honeymoon house – is left unanswered. The dialogue also suggests indecision: the bridegroom invites the man, who is given no more definite identity than 'stranger', to 'look at the sky,/and question' and later declares that he has no answer: 'Stranger, I wish I knew.' The imagery, too, suggests neither one season nor another: from the trees are both fruit and falling leaves and it is 'Autumn, yes', but 'winter was in the wind'.

As the men stand in the porch, the focus shifts to the bride, who is 'in the dusk alone'. Her 'rose-red face' is symbolic of her youthful beauty and – along with 'the thought of her heart's desire', which rhymes with 'bent over the open fire' – suggests the heat of her passion and eagerness to be with the bridegroom to consummate her marriage. Halfway through the stanza, the narrative returns to the bridegroom, whose situation looking 'at the weary road' contrasts with that of his bride by the fireside. Thinking of her provokes one of the poem's most striking images as he:

> ... wished her heart in a case of gold
> And pinned with a silver pin.

Consider this description. Might the beauty and preciousness of the image – with its gold and silver – suggest the value the bridegroom places on his wedding night, which is being devalued by the appearance of the poor stranger? Some may see the desire to pin her heart as symbolic of his desire for sex, with the silver pin as a phallic symbol. Alternatively, readers might find something troubling in the desire to pin her heart and preserve it like a prized exhibit in a scientific museum. Perhaps the image might symbolise a desire to objectify and control: to be able to contain and enjoy a woman's love wherever the male chooses; to be able to enjoy a woman as a decorative item, free from having to consider her as a real person with real needs.

Build critical skills

Consider the similarities of Frost's poem and Coleridge's *The Rime of the Ancient Mariner*. In Coleridge's ballad a stranger (the ancient mariner) approaches a young bridegroom and interrupts his wedding to tell a tale of crime, penance and redemption. By the time the tale has been told, the groom has become a wiser man.

The final stanza might suggest that a compromise is reached: the bridegroom does send the stranger away, but he also helps him: the bridegroom 'thought it little to give/A dole of bread, a purse,/A heartfelt prayer for the poor of God'. Although, some might read the 'he thought it little to give' to mean that he thought about these things rather than he actually did them, and it is possible to read the poem as ending with the stranger on the porch before the groom has decided what to do. Indeed the narrative concludes not with an answer, but with a restating of the question, this time couched in more universal terms:

> But whether or not a man was asked
> To mar the love of two
> By harbouring woe in the bridal house,
> The bridegroom wished he knew.

Charlotte Mew (1869–1928), 'À quoi bon dire' (1916)

The speaker addresses a loved one whom everyone thinks is dead but her. Everyone but the addressee sees that the speaker is old. She imagines a future morning when a couple will kiss and imagine their love is unique, while in the background, the speaker and addressee will smile.

Commentary The poem's French title translates as 'What's the good of saying', or 'What's the point of speaking'. It works by the irony that the reader realises that the loved one has been dead for 17 years, while the speaker behaves as though he is alive. Despite the poem being addressed to a ghost by a woman who is denying present realities, her words do not sound like the ravings of an unsound mind; her tone is gentle and loving, and because the reader only gains information from this subjective perspective he or she is likely to be sympathetic to the speaker and her mode of thought.

The first two quatrains follow the same pattern. Three lines of **iambic tetrameter** establish an idea, then a single line comprised of a single **iamb** draws attention to an alternative way of thinking. Its brevity lends the short line prominence and it is as though the rest of the world is wrong, except the speaker or the addressee. A closeness and harmony between speaker and addressee is also established: everyone thinks the addressee dead, but the speaker; everyone thinks the speaker old, but the addressee.

The final stanza varies the pattern and differs from the first two in that, rather than simply refer to the poem's central relationship, it articulates a wider truth about love. It is also more vivid and descriptive, with an idyllic romantic setting evoked by the 'fine morning in a sunny lane'. Shifting from the present tense of the second stanza, it is expressed in the future and the repeated 'will' also seems to add a sense of certainty to the experience described. The 'boy and the girl', who 'meet and kiss and swear/That nobody can ever love their way again' reflect the feelings of any young couple. The smile of the addressee gently

CRITICAL VIEW

Michael Schmidt writes of Mew that 'She does not write the poem straight out: she assembles it, fits it together. The artistry is in the organisation. Content, under sufficient emotional pressure, will violate form if the poem is to be true ... The emotional content elbows the form out, or draws it in.' (Schmidt, 1998). To what extent might this comment – or parts of this comment – be helpful in understanding 'À Quoi Bon Dire'?

suggests that he and the speaker understand that the young couple's love is far from unique; this smile is balanced by the loving gesture of the speaker who tosses her lover's hair. Note how the stanzaic form alters as the poet makes this final observation: the first three lines that develop the story of the young lovers are in **iambic tetrameter** (lines of eight syllables, divided into four iambic units), while the third short line of **iambic dimeter** (a line of four syllables, divided into two iambic units) slows the pace as the mood shifts and the poem focuses on the older lovers. The rhyme scheme also alters as the fourth line not only rhymes with the fifth but the sixth, reinforcing the sense of finality as the poem closes with the image of the united older lovers as they watch what is perhaps a younger version of themselves.

Louis MacNeice (1907–63), 'Meeting Point' (1939)

A couple meet in a coffee shop; their love is so intense that the world around them seems to stop. The escalator, the bell, the waiter, the clock and so on are all still. The speaker praises God that time can stop in this way. The room was illuminated with one glow because 'Time was away and she was here'.

Commentary MacNeice uses a range of poetic strategies to convey the still and special moment that endures as the lovers meet. The use of repetition in which each stanza begins and ends with the same line and in which the last stanza is a near copy of the first creates cyclical effects; the man and the woman are wrapped up in each other and everything else seems wrapped around them. Each stanza is like a separate enclosed moment within the poem that is itself a closed moment.

Another remarkable quality is the way in which MacNeice takes an ordinary moment – what could be more ordinary than sitting in a cafe? – and makes it seem extraordinary. There is also something special about how he takes a very public place and transforms it into a location for an intensely private interaction. Some believe this expresses a very British sort of reserve, where emotions are deeply felt, but cannot be publicly expressed.

While the poem is largely conventional– with full rhymes and a steady **iambic tetrameter** –the imagery is unusual and arresting. Imagery drawn from modern urban life transforms into the natural; the realistic merges suddenly into the fantastic. Perhaps this novel use of juxtapositioning and blending of opposites owes something to **modernism** (which was an established literary style by the 1930s), or you might see it as having something in common with **metaphysical conceits**. The opening images are plain and emblematic of a meeting in a coffee shop – 'two glasses and two chairs' – but swiftly transform into something magical: 'two people with the one pulse'. The allusion is perhaps to the idea that two people become one when they are truly in love – an idea found in classical texts, such as Plato's *Symposium*, as well as in the Bible and in Shakespeare. Though expressed simply the image gains power through the gentle use of alliteration that links the two 'people' and the one 'pulse', the contrast between the previous three uses of 'two' and the use of 'one' and by the positioning of the line. Centrally located as the third of the five stanzas, it is prominent and rhymes with both the first line and the fifth line. This profoundly human and spiritual moment is enveloped between everyday details: first, of the 'glasses' and 'chairs' and secondly by '(Somebody stopped the moving stairs)'. This latter image is one of modernity and modern culture, which has been put on hold by profound human feeling and an even bigger sense of how the couple are enclosed in their own bubble of timelessness and togetherness, oblivious to the struggles of modern life, suggested by the idea in the sixth stanza when they are described as 'not caring if the markets crash' – a reference to the Wall Street Crash of 1929, which heralded worldwide economic hardship which lasted well into the 1930s.

Much of the imagery transforms from natural to cultural and vice versa. For example, the pastoral image of the stream following through heather – uses imagery drawn from nature to convey the peace and contentment of the couple – calls to mind the flowing of tea or coffee when it becomes 'limpid brown' and we are told that the couple 'sat in a coffee shop'. A similar yet more arresting – even surreal – image follows in the next stanza when 'a bell' (another image of culture and presumably the bell attached to the door that indicates the arrival of more customers) becomes transformed into 'a flower'. It is a beautiful image of time standing still, silence enduring as a moment of togetherness away from the rapid movement of modern life, and its importance is underlined by its recurrence at the very heart of the poem's final stanza.

In the final two stanzas, MacNeice expands on the implications of the enduring joyful moment. The divine, which was implicit in the earlier image of the radio waltz coming out 'like water from a rock', is made explicit: 'God or whatever means the good/Be praised that time can stop like this'. This moment is worth celebrating, worth giving thanks for, and MacNeice explains the effects of that moment: there is a sense of deep understanding (perceived by the heart) and the body feels a deep sense of peace. The moment of transformation – which, as we have noted, is evoked throughout in images of transformation – means that life is 'no longer what is was' and the whole room is radiant as a consequence:

And all the room one glow because
Time was away and she was here.

Context

```
The simile of the music of the waltz coming from the
radio like water from a rock is an allusion to the Bible
(Exodus 17:3-7). In the wilderness the Israelites are so
thirsty they are about to turn on their leader, Moses. God
instructs Moses to take his staff and strike it on a rock
in front of three elders of the Church. He does so, water
flows and Moses warns his people not to doubt God again.
```

Build critical skills

Sharpen your critical appreciation of 'Meeting Point' by comparing it to 'In a Bath Tea Shop', a poem written by **John Betjeman** in 1945. You can search to find a copy of the poem online.

Taking it further ▶

The broadcaster and writer Clive James offers the following assessment of the poem:

he has precisely tapped into the perennial British conviction (stand by for Brief Encounter*) that heterosexual love between adults should reach its emotional apotheosis at a public meeting point where the most intense thoughts must stay unspoken, with the world crowding around to stifle the passion.*

(Clive James, *Reading for Life*, www.clivejames.com/poetry-notebook/5)

Explain James' view and explore the extent to which you agree with him. Use the internet to find out more about *Brief Encounter* (1945).

Keith Douglas (1920–44) '*Vergissmeinnicht*' (1943)

Three weeks after a battle, a British tank crew return to the place where a German gun had attacked. In the gunpit they see both a dead gunner and a picture of his girlfriend who has written her name, Steffi, and '*Vergissmeinnicht*' (Forget-me-not). The speaker reflects on Steffi's probable reactions to seeing her boyfriend's body and the poem concludes with thoughts about the soldier and the lover being mingled in the same body and how Death, who has singled out the soldier, has also killed the lover.

Commentary The poem is a heart-breaking meditation on the nature of war and its effects on love. The power of its emotion moves us to sympathise with an enemy gunner and, in particular, his unseen girlfriend – so much so that, by the end, we have transcended the World War II context and the German gunner has become so much more than an enemy. Indeed his two main identities have separated and become archetypes: 'the soldier', and 'the lover' to whom 'death' has done 'a mortal hurt'.

The poem begins with a narrative of the British tank crew returning to their former place of battle. After a matter-of-fact start, details draw our attention: it is amongst 'the nightmare ground' that they find the place of intense fighting and our attention is drawn to the body of a dead German gunner. The **internal rhyme** of 'ground' and 'found' and the repetition of the latter rhyming word make the reader sit up and notice the 'soldier sprawling in the sun'. Alliteration alerts us to the uncomfortable position in which the German lies, and he becomes the poem's central subject.

In the third quatrain, the language grows personal. Rather than retain the relatively distant perspective of the opening, the narrator begins with a single word imperative sentence: 'Look.' The reader's attention focuses on a small detail: a picture of the German gunner's girlfriend; expressing the feelings of the one in the photograph and the one to whom it was given, the picture is 'dishonoured'; it is also inscribed by the name of the name of the person it depicts, Steffi, and her instruction: '*Vergissmeinnicht*'. We have a sense of the care she has taken with the photograph: her name and the inscription have been written 'in a copybook Gothic script'.

The fourth quatrain contrasts with the third: the focus returns to the British tank crew, who see the dead German 'almost with content'; rather than mourn, they almost feel satisfied at his death, which is hardly surprising, since – as we discovered in the second stanza – three weeks previously he had hit their tank with a shell that felt like 'the entry of a demon'. Yet the worst humiliation comes not from the British soldiers, but the gunner's own equipment. There is something phallic about the shape of a gun, which seems to mock him, and is 'hard and good': the erect and fully-functioning gun contrasts with the 'decayed' former lover, who will never see his Steffi again, much less make love to her.

The penultimate stanza returns to focus on Steffi, allowing the reader to imagine her suffering if she were to see his dead body which has lain decomposing in the heat of the desert for three weeks. Images like the 'swart flies' moving on his skin, the 'dust on his paper eye/and the burst stomach like a cave' render the corpse in vivid detail and create an emotional impact on the reader, making us sympathise both with the dead soldier and, especially, with his girlfriend.

In the final stanza, the poem's scope broadens from the intimate details of the soldier's body to consider him in universalised terms: he now represents both 'the lover and the killer'. The two-syllable full rhyme in the first and third line with 'mingled' and 'singled' helps to add impact to the ideas of blended identities and the definite though random act of fate. In a poem whose metre has largely followed the rhythms of speech, the second and final lines of the final stanza stand out as the reader is carried along by the force of two perfectly balanced lines of **iambic tetrameter**. The final half rhyme on 'heart' and 'hurt' sounds a mournful note and makes us think of the heartbreak that the death has caused.

Context

Keith Douglas served in North Africa as a Tank Commander during World War II. His writing reveals premonitions of his death. Ted Hughes notes how, in April 1944, his final poem noted that:

> *The next month, then, is a window*
> *and with a crash I'll split the glass.*
> *Behind it stands one I must kiss,*
> *person of love or death,*
> *a person or a wraith,*
> *I fear what I shall find.*

Hughes then reports that 'On the morning 9 June 1944, when a mortar fragmentation bomb exploded in a tree above him, he was killed by a splinter so fine that no wound showed on his body.' (Graham (ed.), 1990)

Build critical skills

Think about what it means to do someone hurt, then consider the final main clause of the poem: 'death ... / has done the lover mortal hurt'. For what reasons does Douglas describe the death of the German soldier in this way; why does he not state it more directly?

Philip Larkin (1922–85), 'Wild Oats' (1963)

The speaker narrates the story of meeting two women: one was attractive; the other, he felt comfortable talking to. He and the second one courted for seven years, but their engagement was broken off. The attractive woman was met twice more, but the speaker thought she was secretly laughing at him. He reflects on the aspects of his personality that led to the break up, such as his selfishness. The poem closes on two pictures in his wallet: they are of the attractive woman wearing fur gloves.

Commentary 'Wild Oats' casts an ironic eye on courtship, debunking the myths that people choose soul mates and that men enjoy sexual adventures before settling down. The speaker is a forlorn figure, who describes the woman who is out of his league with much more gusto than the one he spent seven years with. Love in the poem seems to be represented in two unsatisfactory ways: a repressed desire for what can never be gained and which only finds release in secretive, smutty humour; or a resignation that you should settle for what you can get, even if it's ultimately dull and joyless. What is perhaps most interesting, though, is the ambiguity in the presentation of the speaker. How seriously do we take him? Perhaps, rather than laugh we might find pathos behind the mocking self-pity and perhaps admire Larkin for bravely showing us that love does not always give lives meaning and happiness.

The story is told in a down-to-earth manner, with colloquial idioms and turns of phrase, the narrative drawing our attention to the beautiful woman, whom we perhaps expect to be the co-star of the love story, until our expectations are humorously overturned in the eighth line: 'But it was the friend I took out'. Other aspects are humorous too, such as the juxtaposed images of the two women:

> A bosomy English rose
> And her friend in specs I could talk to

While some might object to women being defined by breasts or glasses, or indeed the generic 'English rose' label, others might see the comedy in the ridiculous image, which is perhaps reminiscent of a scene on a saucy seaside postcard of the 1950s or 60s. There is also a comic clash of sound, between **assonance** and the long vowel sounds of 'bosomy English rose' and the harsh consonants and sibilance of 'friend in specs'; in addition, the final part of the second description might be seen as quite touching if we consider a biographical reading (see the Context feature opposite) in which feeling comfortable with a woman is an important part of courtship.

The second stanza's long first sentence, with phrases such as 'seven years', over 'four hundred letters' and a 'ten guinea ring' miserably enumerating the time and money spent on the relationship, culminates in a sense of pointlessness: they met in cathedral cities 'unknown to the clergy'. The short

Context

Larkin never married. In 1951 he wrote to a friend: 'I find it amazingly difficult to talk to girls – not through shyness, so much as ignorance and apathy. I don't know what to talk to them about and really don't make much of a job of the old parlour tricks. Unless a girl is ½-way to meet me I am nowhere.' (Burnett (ed.), 2012) sentence that follows – saying that he 'met beautiful twice' – shifts the pace as the tone grows more serious and the speaker reveals that 'She was trying/ Both times (so I thought) not to laugh'. The implication that the woman was mocking the speaker or felt his attentions risible seems powerfully felt by the speaker; the phrase in brackets suggests this is something he has dwelt on and its position at the end of the stanza allows its impact on the reader to linger.

It almost seems that the speaker decides to 'snap out of it' in the final stanza as he masks uncomfortable thoughts of the unattainable woman with more humour arising from the relationship that ended. His list of the qualities that made him unsuited to love begin sounding self-critical, but with too 'easily bored', end with an implied criticism of his former fiancée. The poem closes by returning to 'beautiful' and the image of two photographs – both of 'bosomy English rose with fur gloves on'. While you might find the idea of a man carrying, for 20 years, pictures of a woman who rejected him somewhat perverse, the last line might summon up some sympathy for this speaker whose final thoughts – 'unlucky charms, perhaps' – sound lingering notes of self-doubt, vulnerability and disappointment.

Philip Larkin (1922–85), 'Talking in Bed' (1964)

Reflecting on the situation of a couple in bed, the speaker suggests that this should be the most conducive situation for communication; the couple, however, are more and more silent. Outside, the weather is unsettled. The external world seems disconnected from the couple, and the poem concludes on the thought that it is difficult for the couple to find anything to say to each other – anything that is either honest or sympathetic.

Commentary The poem's point of view is interesting. At once distanced and close, the first seven lines appear to be from the perspective of an observer who muses on the situation of two people lying in bed together, but the eighth, which starts with the sentence 'None of this cares for us.', suggests that the speaker is one of the two people.

The poem communicates disconnectedness: both the people in the bed from each other and this couple from the rest of the world. In the first stanza, they are not 'two people being honest', but 'an emblem' of this. In the second, the unsettled weather mirrors the couple's mood; as Christopher Ricks points out, 'the wind's incomplete unrest' alludes gloomily to the easy restfulness of 'a complete rest' (Burnett, 2012). The 'dark towns [that] heap up on the horizon' in the third stanza suggest the couple's alienation, not only from each other but also the world, an idea confirmed the sentence that follows it: 'None of this cares for us.'

By the final stanza the poem returns to explore directly the subject broached in the first: the difficulty of talking in bed. Moving from the wide open spaces of weather and landscape to the intimate personal space of the bed, the last sentence articulates a paradox: there is no explanation for the phenomenon that despite being so physically close – 'At this unique distance from isolation' – the couple find it increasingly hard to communicate kindly or honestly.

Note how Larkin's conclusion includes a plethora of negation: the middle line of the penultimate stanza expresses both 'None' and 'Nothing'; in the final line, the poem culminates in a cluster of negatives as the couple can neither find 'Words at once true and kind,/Or **not un**true and **not un**kind'. The repetition links both sound and sense as the ideas are repeated and internal half rhymes on 'once true' and 'untrue', 'and kind' with 'unkind' – help the ideas to linger in the reader's mind. The final line's subtle wording, with its carefully-phrased indirect statement using two double negatives, might evoke a relationship in which words need to be chosen with extreme care to avoid causing offense or misunderstanding. Words that are 'not untrue' are not outright lies, but they might contain elements of deception; those that are 'not unkind' might on the surface seem to be pleasant, but they might not be completely friendly or innocent either. This points to the bitter irony of the title: the poem entitled 'Talking in Bed' is actually about the difficulties of doing just that.

Taking it further ▶

To what extent do you agree with the following statement:

'Rather than being a gloomy observer, who looks down on others, Larkin is a passionate poet, whose verse is concerned with real people and real emotions.'

CRITICAL VIEW

Larkin was influenced by Hardy; he admired Hardy's pronouncements or sayings (what he terms dicta) about poetry:

All those wonderful dicta about poetry: 'the poet should touch our hearts by showing his own', 'the poet takes note of nothing that he cannot feel', 'the emotion of all the ages and the thought of his own' – Hardy knew what it was all about.

(Philip Larkin, 'Philip Larkin, The Art of Poetry No. 30,' *The Paris Review*, 1982)

How far do you find the above ideas helpful in your study of Larkin's verse?

Elizabeth Jennings (1926–2001), 'One Flesh' (1966)

The speaker describes an old couple in separate beds, doing different things: he reading, she looking at the ceiling. It is as though they are the remnants from a previous love; the atmosphere is cold; they no longer have physical contact. They face sexlessness for the rest of their lives. Though apart and silent, they are near in terms of proximity. The speaker wonders if they know they are old and reveals herself to be their daughter.

Commentary The poem appears to be in the third person, until the last stanza when we discover that, far from being a distant or omniscient depiction, the poem has been written from the perspective of the couple's daughter. It opens by reflecting on the relationship between the old couple, in which they are emotionally distant. The imagery in the first stanza establishes this situation: they lie in separate beds; he seems to be reading, while she looks at the ceiling above. Yet things seem worse. He only looks like he's reading –'the book he holds [is] unread' – while she affixes her gaze on 'the shadows overhead'. The couplet, which might help to sound a note of unity, paradoxically, serves to reinforce their being together in their separateness. Things look more gloomy if we think that the unread book is an ineffective means to stave off boredom, or, worse, a way for him to avoid having to speak to his wife. Similarly, the staring at the shadows could suggest boredom on the part of the wife, or it might convey a sinister subtext – perhaps all she can foresee is gloominess, or she only looks forward to death.

As the speaker develops her reflections in the second stanza, the fading of physical love is a primary concern. 'Flotsam' means the goods washed up after a shipwreck, and this is how they are described: the leftovers after an old passion. More than this, the potential antipathy hinted at in the first stanza recurs as their infrequent touches are said to indicate either no strong feeling '– or too much.' A sense of barely suppressed dislike is reinforced by the **caesura**, the **end-stop** and by the way in which the phrase finishes the stanza's long central sentence. The couplet reinforces the depressing message:

> Chastity faces them, a destination
> For which their whole lives were a preparation.

Note how the couplet uses longer lines of 11 syllables; this means that each line ends on an unstressed syllable (a **feminine ending**). Feminine endings have a falling rhythm and are sometimes used to suggest a subtle sense of disappointment – especially in a poem like this one in which the vast majority of the lines have a rising rhythm (or **masculine ending**) as they end on a stressed syllable. Look at the rhyme too: the sense of their whole lives as leading up to this outcome is reinforced by a rhyme that utilises not one syllable, but four ('destination'/'preparation'). The meaning of the lines is paradoxical: we normally associate sexlessness as the state of a single person before marriage, rather than the outcome of being married. Sexlessness seems more prominent too as the first word of the stanza's penultimate line and by it being termed 'chastity' – a state associated with holy orders entered into to bring one closer to God – gives it an inflated sense of importance. It being a 'destination' also gives it an air of inevitability and perhaps broadens the idea of a passionless life in old age as the fated end of all couples.

Biblical language is used elsewhere to add solemnity – or gentle humour – to the couple's situation. Confession, is, of course, a Roman Catholic sacrament in which the sinner admits a sin to the priest, demonstrates that he or she is truly sorry and is eventually given absolution – that is, spiritual cleansing and forgiveness. In the case of the couple, their touches are compared to confessions that they either don't feel enough for each other, or else feel too much (which might suggest that they feel annoyance or anger). The title itself is biblical. The idea that man and woman are joined and become one flesh – that is a single unit – is perhaps gently mocked by the poem. Indeed the first phrase of the poem might show this. In the Bible to lie often means to have sex with and 'Lying apart now' and 'apart' can mean removed from consideration, so it is clear at the outset that the couple, though married, are certainly not one flesh.

There is, however, one other important person in the relationship: the speaker. The final stanza opens: 'Strangely apart, yet strangely close together'. She is the one who dwells on the paradox of their closeness yet apartness and how strange this is. The speaker uses thread as a simile to evoke the silence between them. There is a sense of fragility, though an undeniable sense of connectedness. The feather that she uses for time might suggest the imperceptible way that a relationship grows cold or how people age. The final sentence acquires additional impact by the way in which it breaks the established stanzaic form:

> ... Do they know they're **old**,
> These two who are my father and my mother
> Whose fire from which I came, has now grown **cold**?

The reader's final impression is of the strangeness of the relationship: not the paradox of closeness yet separateness that has run throughout the poem, but the sense of the fire of passion that has been extinguished. We are denied the pleasure of a couplet that adds a conclusive answer; instead we are given a rhyme that reaches back to the idea of the couple and the question of whether or not they recognise they are old.

Ending with an interrogative is appropriate in another way, for we might question the extent to which the speaker can really know the intimate thoughts and feelings of her parents; indeed many of the daughter's comments are hedged with terms such as 'it is as if' or other comparisons. Perhaps some of the strangeness and discomfort at their relationship comes from the speaker herself. After all, many of us feel uncomfortable at the thought of our parents having sex, and this is the poem's central topic. Might it be that the younger woman projects her thoughts on to the older couple who may not be thinking in those terms? Perhaps the natural state of being a couple might not be a depressing cooling of desire; perhaps a couple can love, or feel companionship, in a different way. It is difficult to discern much hope in Jennings' poem, and the couple might only be held by a thread, but, at least, you might argue, they are together.

Anne Sexton (1928–74) 'For My Lover, Returning to His Wife' (1968)

A mistress reflects on her lover's wife. The wife is solid, domestic and permanent like a sculpture made for her husband, while the mistress feels she is a momentary luxury, like a red boat in the harbour. The wife's roles are considered, from making a beautiful home to bearing and caring for three children. The mistress accepts the husband's return to his wife and thinks of the sex and the intimacy that there will be between the couple. While the wife is solid, like a monument, the mistress will 'wash off' like a watercolour.

Commentary 'For My Lover, Returning to His Wife' was first published in the famous American literary magazine, *The New Yorker* on 3 February 1968. In many ways, it shows the dark side of the sexual revolution: the increased sexual opportunities afforded sound like a great liberation, but perhaps when these opportunities reach married adults in the suburbs, they liberate some more than others. It is interesting to reflect on who gains most from the love triangle of husband – mistress – wife. The husband gains the luxury and excitement of the affair and can return to the stability of his wife, while the mistress must deal with the emotional fallout of being disposable. The poem draws heavily on autobiographical material dealing with the above issues and more as it dramatises the intimate thoughts and feelings of the mistress in a direct and immediate manner that is unconstrained by metrical or stanzaic patterns. This type of work became known as **confessional poetry** and Sexton is perhaps its most celebrated practitioner.

Despite its **free verse** and freely flowing, emotional style, the poem is incredibly well crafted. Notice, for instance, the imagery of art at both the beginning and the end of the poem. First the wife is compared to a commissioned sculpture; this woman's identity has been fragmented and recast specifically for her husband: 'she was/melted carefully down' for him. The connections are strong, since she is not only associated with the present and adult life, but also with the past and his childhood: she has been 'cast up from [his] one hundred favorite aggies'. This simile can be read as the wife having been formed by the melting and recasting of his toy marbles ('aggies' as in marbles made from agate); this is not only an image of transformation and of childhood becoming adulthood but one that carries a sense of the colours and texture of a marble statue. A commissioned piece of art is not something that is seen, desired and bought, but something that is created especially for a particular person.

▲ '… from your one hundred favourite aggies'

By the end of the poem, the references to art show that the wife has gained stature and solidity: she has expanded from marble statue to 'monument' – she is a piece of personal and public art that commemorates and memorialises. The poem's poignant ending shows that the mistress, however, is not made from marble or rock, but the impermanent and cheaper material of watercolour paint:

> As for me, I am a watercolor.
> I wash off.

There is also a hint of the physicality of the affair and of the husband's guilt. Washing is often associated with spiritual cleansing and the final three lines may refer to the idea that the husband, having spent time with his mistress,

Build critical skills

Think of the ways in which the wife and her marital roles are presented. While there are images of domesticity, such as the 'cast iron pot', there are also images of excitement, such as 'Fireworks in the dull middle of February' (which may refer to sex and celebrations on Valentine's Day). Then consider those that refer to the mistress, such as the 'bright red sloop' (a sailing boat) and 'Littleneck clams out of season'. How does Sexton make you respond to each woman?

can simply shower away the evidence of their sex and return to his wife clean and untroubled by his deception.

It is interesting to reflect on the subject matter of the poem. Rather than being preoccupied with the direct expression of her own feelings for their relationship, the speaker seems to be more concerned with the relationship of the husband and his wife – and is particularly interested in his wife.

Note, however, the shift in tone, when the poem slows to the lines:

> I give you back your heart.
> I give you permission –

While they seem calm and reasonable, they augur a storm of emotions as the speaker moves from the reasoned thoughts of the wife's devotion to her children to more fragmented and angry images, such as 'for the bitch in her' and 'for the burying of her small red wound alive'. It seems that images of the wife's sexuality are troubling to consider and while, rationally, the speaker seems to feel no ill will toward the wife, there is a kind of visceral response to her situation that produces something closer to hate.

The final images before the juxtaposition of the monument and the watercolour include those of the husband's sexual feelings for his wife: there is an animalistic aspect as 'the call' – or instinct for sex – is obeyed:

> when you will burrow in arms and breasts
> and tug at the orange ribbon in her hair
> and answer the call, the curious call.

Yet this is almost a nesting instinct as well as a sexual one: the husband will 'burrow' like an animal going into its home – a hiding place, a place of security. The sexual images of the 'arms and breasts' are also maternal ones and the 'orange ribbon' lends an air of wholesome prettiness to the encounter.

'For My Lover, Returning to His Wife' is a remarkable poem for the way that the autobiographical speaker recognises the many-faceted nature of the relationship of the husband and wife, and, while it is a **confessional poem**, it does not wallow in selfish feelings, but rather lays bare the complexities of a situation for the reader. The result is that he or she is likely to feel sympathy for the speaker and appreciate the pain and emotional complications arising from adultery.

Seamus Heaney (1939–2013), 'Punishment' (1975)

The poem expresses the thoughts and feelings of the speaker as he considers the well-preserved exhumed body of an Iron Age woman, who has been executed for adultery. He scrutinises her body and the bog from which it came, then considers the beauty she would have had before her punishment. He feels something like love for her but recognises that he would have been silent in the face of those who were intent on killing her. He has stood by while other women have meted out punishment, and while he feels just anger at such treatment, he understands the need on the part of the punishers to exact revenge.

Commentary The speaker evokes two different, though related experiences: the execution of an Iron Age woman for adultery and the tarring and feathering of a Northern Irish Catholic woman for her relationship with a British soldier in the 1970s. The experiences not only have similarities in terms of the imagery to do with young women with shaved heads being immersed in tar-like fluids, but the poet might also use them to explore an equivalence between the harsh tribal laws of the Iron Age and those of the divided communities in Northern Ireland. Perhaps, Heaney seems to be suggesting, there is an atavistic need to protect the tribe and to punish those who threaten it from within that persists no matter how civilised we think we become.

The first part of the poem – as the final line of the eighth stanza recognises – is voyeuristic. The speaker casts his eyes over the exhumed body in a debased version of a **blazon**, deriving pleasure as he looks at sexual parts of her body, such as 'the nape of her neck', 'her naked front' and 'her nipples'. At first the poem is mysterious: the loving tone seems at odds with the subject matter as we realise gradually that the speaker is viewing the preserved body of one who has been executed. There is a paradoxical mix of the violent and the erotic as the speaker gently comments on the body, revealing a situation where love has led to death – an idea that is poetically encapsulated in the image of 'her noose' which is 'a ring to store/the memories of love'.

Taking it further ▷

Carry out research into the images that inspired Heaney's bog poems. While several come from pictures of bodies recovered from Danish bogs (see P.V. Glob's *The Bog People*), it is thought that the particular body that Heaney had in mind when writing 'Punishment' was Windeby I from North Germany. You can find pictures of this body if you conduct an internet image search, typing Windeby I into the search engine.

▲ One of the images (of a body found in the Iron Age peat bog) that inspired Heaney

After the loving feelings towards the victim culminate in the image of her former beauty and the statement 'My poor scapegoat,/I almost love you', the poem turns on the contrastive conjunction 'but' and the speaker places himself more centrally in the poem to interrogate not only the situation – which merges subtly into that of a Northern Irish woman being tarred and feathered – but also his own responses, which he admits are morally ambiguous. For example, despite his loving feelings, he knows he would 'have cast ... /the stones of silence'. Note the hushed sibilance of the admission, the paradox of silence being thrown and the biblical allusion.

TASK

The allusion in the eighth stanza is to the Bible: John 8: 7. A woman who has committed adultery is taken out for public punishment and Jesus is asked to comment on the law that says an adulteress should be punished by stoning. Jesus replies: 'He that is without sin among you, let him first cast a stone at her'.

Using the poem and the biblical allusion, explain the implied criticism of the speaker.

The imagery grows more realistic after the ninth stanza, which the admission of the speaker being an 'artful voyeur'; the setting is clearly not Iron Age Denmark but 1970s Northern Ireland:

> I who have stood dumb
> when your betraying sisters,
> cauled in tar,
> wept by the railings,

The 'betraying sisters' are those in the Catholic community who believe the younger woman has betrayed her community through her relationship with a British soldier and administer her punishment. Heaney renders them as the betrayers (not the victim, who, arguably, has betrayed her community); note also how Heaney's speaker – no matter how emotionally he is affected by the events – 'stood dumb' and did nothing.

Complex and paradoxical thoughts and feelings overwhelm the speaker in the final stanza. He recognises that he is one

> Who would connive
> in civilised outrage
> yet understand the exact
> and tribal intimate revenge.

Many have questioned Heaney's stance in the poem. While Edna Longley recognises that 'the paradox "connive . . . civilised" is designed to corner people who think they have risen above the primitive', she wonders if the poet can simultaneously identify with both the victim and those who punish her (Longley, 1996).

Of course it is also possible to think of Heaney as being brave enough to voice the feelings of the silent majority: those who oppose violence as a means to a political end in Northern Ireland, but when they encounter sectarianism are perhaps too timid or too complacent to do more than turn a blind eye. The feelings of understanding for those who punish that close the poem are both uncomfortable and uncomfortably convincing. They seem more fully realised than the earlier, more generic feelings of outrage and, in this vacillating poem, they have the last word. It is a last word that resonates disturbingly: the speaker seems to admit to himself that there is something strict, precise and fitting about this 'exact and tribal, intimate revenge'.

CRITICAL VIEW

Ciaran Carson suggests that Heaney 'seems to be offering his "understanding" of the situation almost as a consolation … It is if he is saying that suffering like this is natural' (Longley, 1996). In your own words, explain the critics' main objections to Heaney's stance in 'Punishment' and the extent to which you believe they are justified.

Tony Harrison (born 1937), 'Timer' (1978)

The speaker reflects on his mother's wedding ring, which has been returned by post after her cremation. He remembers his father's instruction to ensure that the ring was cremated with her. Looking at the ring in his hand, he imagines his mother's ashes passing through it – like the sands in the egg timer he used to watch as a boy.

Commentary This touching lyric is written in the form of a **Meredithian sonnet** – a sonnet of 16 lines usually comprised of four quatrains. It explores two types of love: the love of the son for his dead mother and the love of the father for his wife. The story is divided into three parts. The first and the last are each comprised of four lines in the present tense concerning the unburnable wedding ring. The second (of eight lines) is in the past tense and is a recollection of the speaker's experience at the crematorium.

While written using simple language narrating a story of 'ordinary' working-class people there is something extraordinary about the emotions and feelings described in the poem and in the power and depth of the love they share. Two ordinary objects – a ring and an egg timer – assume symbolic, almost mythical, proportions. The poem's very first word describes the ring, and its importance is suggested straight away. 'Gold' is a stressed syllable in a poem that otherwise starts each line with an **iamb**; it forces the reader to linger and the idea of this precious metal and that it 'survives the fire that's hot enough/To make you ashes' makes it seem magical. Its magic in the first two lines is also suggested not only through the contrast with its packaging of 'coarse official buff', but also through its inscription of the names of the couple and it being

Context

The Meredithian sonnet is named after the Victorian poet George Meredith (1828-1909), whose *Modern Love* (1862) is a sequence of 16-line sonnets, which chart the break up of his marriage.

termed an 'eternity' – a common name for a type of ring, but in this context one suggestive of its symbolic function as an emblem of a love that will last for ever. This is something the speaker's father feels strongly about when he instructs him that the ring must be burnt with his wife – it is 'his surety that they'd be together, "later"'.

The way in which the poem is structured also gives prominence to the ring. It is the subject of both the first and the last four lines, which means that the eight lines of the central section – a recollection of the speaker's experience in the crematorium – are encircled by images of the ring. The last four are particularly interesting. The poem's only single line stanza is an awestruck **exclamatory sentence**: 'It's on my warm palm now your burnished ring!' Note how the word 'burnished' stands out as both the only **polysyllabic** word in this line of monosyllables and as an unusual, archaic-sounding adjective in this poem containing a mostly simple vocabulary. Burnished makes the ring sound like a polished, shining and perfectly-crafted object from the Middle Ages (a sense that might remind us of the mythical-sounding opening of 'Gold survives the fire'). The magic that it emits is evoked in the final three lines as the ring image merges into the circle in the centre of the egg timer; note how the words 'circle slowly' take up a central position in this stanza giving the reader a visual image of the circle at the heart of the timer:

> I feel your ashes, head, arms, breasts, womb, legs,
> sift through its **circle slowly**, like that thing
> you used to let me watch to time the eggs.

It is interesting how Harrison has taken a symbol of eternity and placed it in the centre of a symbol of transience. In addition, there is a sense of familial love as the image of romantic love between a couple has become part of an image of filial love as the adult son looks back with affection on the homely scene of watching the egg timer with his mother. Not only this, but the imagery is made even more richly ambiguous when we remember that the poem's last word – 'eggs' – is also symbolic of new birth.

Paul Muldoon (born 1951), 'Long Finish' (1998)

The speaker addresses his wife, reflecting on their marriage ceremony under a canopy in the middle of a wood. They share white wine and the speaker jokes about his desires for her and the ups and downs of parenthood and their ten-year marriage. He looks at a patch of eczema on his wife's shoulder, which makes him think of a line between 'longing and loss'; this somehow summons images from conflict-torn Northern Ireland: terrorists wait in a trench for, then open fire on, a farmer; another farmer is, it seems, about to be blown up by a landmine. The sense of what lies between longing and loss brings him to think of characters from the Japanese Noh play, *Matsukaze*, in which the **eponymous** character's name means 'pine', both in the sense of the tree and in the sense of waiting and yearning. The speaker watches his wife's blouse slip lower, barely covering the eczema, and turns to her and exhorts them not to make distinctions between what's his and what's hers and for them to carry on loving one another passionately.

Commentary Muldoon is known for his technical accomplishments including his intricate uses of rhyme and puns, so it is perhaps fitting that this tender poem, which celebrates a decade of marriage, is written in the intricate and challenging form of the **ballade**. It is a double ballade: all the odd numbered stanzas conclude with one refrain and comprise one ballade, while all the even numbered ones conclude with a different refrain and comprise another ballade. The last stanza's first four lines form a postscript to one ballade and the final four lines performs the same function for the other. Using this French form from the fourteenth and fifteenth centuries, Muldoon opens by addressing the poet's ruler – in this case his wife, whom he later humorously dubs The Princess of Accutane (which sounds like a Medieval French kingdom, but refers to the medicine she uses to treat her eczema). The speaker uses consciously archaic diction in this section as he instructs: 'Save me, good thou,/a piece of marchpane' (marzipan). In keeping with the form, all but the last of the poem's stanzas are **octaves** and include a **refrain**, which in the first stanza is 'and then some'. This creates an amusing close to the first stanza and gives a sense of how the speaker has an excess of blessing in his marriage as he fills his wife's

> ...glass with Simi
> Chardonnay as high as decency allows
> and then some.

Wine also provides the poem's title, since 'long finish' is the term given to the lingering flavour on the palate after a wine has been swallowed. Perhaps this suggests the enjoyment of the marriage, which continues to give pleasure long after the honeymoon.

The second stanza moves playfully along with puns and word associations as the speaker asks his wife to 'Bear with' him while he 'must bear the scrutiny' of the wine, then goes on to use the language of the connoisseur to describe its 'hints of plum and pear,/its muscadine/tempered by an oak backbone'. The metaphorical oak backbone of the wine leads to the metaphorical 'willow-boss' of his wife's breast on which he has 'designs' and 'on all [her] waist confines/ between longing and loss'.

As well as through word play and verbal dexterity, the poet presents love in a mature and all-encompassing way. In addition to noticing physical details such as her breast or her falling blouse, the speaker pays attention to imperfections such as the 'all-but-cleared-up eczema patch' on her back. Marriage is not presented as a plateau of contentment; the speaker compares its highs and lows to the New York stock exchange as he marvels at how he and his wife have 'withstood/the soars and slumps in the Dow/of ten years of marriage and parenthood'. Their decade of marriage is described in oxymoronic terms as 'five years of bitter rapture, five of blissful rows', but the refrain – 'and then some' – allows his thoughts to spill into the fourth stanza and conclude this line of thought by referring to the one or two years when they were 'firmly on cloud nine'.

The fifth and sixth stanzas are unusual in that the speaker's mind drifts from marriage to scenes from the poet's home country of Northern Ireland. The eczema on his wife's back summons thoughts of a trench covered in pine boughs (the detail both looks back to the earlier description of the pine boughs and the pine wood of the couple's wedding and forward to the references to the Japanese character whose name is 'wind in the pines'). Here terrorists lie in wait for a cattle farmer and kill him by semi-automatic rifle fire. In turn, this makes him think of another farmer 'who'll shortly divine/the precise whereabouts of a land mine'. While the reader most likely assumes the farmer is about to be killed by a landmine, Muldoon's punning language makes it possible to think he is about to locate it by means of the ancient art of dowsing.

The chain of associations continues, linking the 'forbearance in the face of' changes of the farmers and the sisters, Murasami (Autumn Rain) and Matsukaze (Pining Wind), who farm salt and await the return of Yukihira, the poet-courtier who wooed them both in the Japanese Noh play, *Matsukaze*.

The final stanza is a postscript (which in the ballade form is called an envoi). It begins as the form dictates, with an address to the poet's ruler. The speaker urges himself and his wife not to make distinctions between good and mediocre wines, between what's hers or what's his, or – using one of the refrains – 'between longing and loss'. The final lines instruct them to have the blind faith of the sisters in the Noh play and live 'with such force and fervour as spouses may yet espouse,/and then some.'

Taking it further ▷

The fifth and sixth stanzas contain images of violence in Northern Ireland. In the months before Muldoon's tenth wedding anniversary (in August 1997), tensions escalated. Marches organised by the Orange Order (the organisation that parades to commemorate the Protestant victory at the Battle of the Boyne in 1690) were highly contentious, and many Catholics objected to marches taking place near them. The biggest dispute was in the town of Muldoon's birth, Portadown; when a march was sanctioned, violence spread. In 36 hours of violence there were 548 attacks on the police and army; 46 were injured and 57 civilians were hurt. To find out more, carry out internet searches for the 1997 riots in Northern Ireland.

Wendy Cope (born 1945), 'After the Lunch' (2002)

After a lunch, the speaker and her loved one say goodbye on Waterloo Bridge. It is cold and windy; the conditions make her eyes water. She tries to suppress the recognition that she is in love. Her rational mind explains away the loving feelings, but her emotions suggest otherwise and she wonders when such instincts were ever wrong. The wind blows in her hair and she feels like skipping. Before she is half way over, she admits that, while her head and her heart say different things, the heart has the upper hand.

Commentary Wendy Cope chooses a romantic location for her poem that explores the feelings of young love. It is a well-known place in London, which – thanks to its position on a bend of the Thames – affords views of landmarks like the Houses of Parliament, the London Eye and Canary Wharf and it features in many films, books and songs.

▲ Waterloo Bridge

The situation is also full of romantic connotations. Usually, lunch is a functional meal taken in the middle of the working day, but here it has been a romantic occasion, with wine – or other alcohol – and witty conversation. This along with the irrepressible feeling of love gives the situation a sense of a special occasion. Cope keeps details of the man and the meal undefined, instead focusing on the feelings of the woman as she walks over the bridge, which as we have seen through its previous uses in **popular culture** is redolent of romance, beauty and excitement. Yet the romance presented by Cope is an accessible one involving a real person, rather than a character played by a film star. The 'black woolly glove' with which the speaker wipes her tears – which may be caused by

Context

Robert E. Sherwood's play *Waterloo Bridge* (1930) was filmed in 1934, 1940 and 1956; it tells of a soldier who marries a woman he met on the bridge during an air raid in World War I.

Context

The influential 1966 film, *Alfie* (a romantic comedy/drama starring Michael Caine), uses the bridge as a location in both its opening and ending sequences. It is also the vantage point from which the singer sees London in the song 'Waterloo Sunset' (1967) by The Kinks.

TASK

Explore the ways in which the title and its associations shape the poem's meaning and create effects.

warm feelings of love as much as cold blasts of wind – are the only descriptive detail of the speaker and they are hardly glamorous.

Perhaps that is Cope's point: she is presenting love as something extraordinary that happens to ordinary people. Her poetic methods are in keeping with this. For example, she uses a vocabulary of common and mostly simple words and a mostly regular metre and rhyme scheme. Look at the first stanza: it is a quatrain – an apt stanzaic form for developing a story – which has a regular aa, bb rhyme and which uses a regular metre. Each line begins with an **iamb**, then follows an **anapaestic** beat:

> On WAT-er-loo BRIDGE, where we SAID our good-BYES

The only exceptions to this pattern are lines six, seven and the last line, which each have an extra syllable and are fully anapaestic. This anapaestic rhythm – with its two light beats followed by a heavy beat – creates a gentle rhythm, appropriate for the poem of gentle realisation about love and about the precedence that loving feelings have over rational doubts.

It is interesting to consider the poem as a down-to-earth example of a struggle within the self. Note how the inner voice of caution is expressed in italics to keep it distinct and give it a sense of insistent intrusion: '*This is nothing. You're high on the charm and the drink.*' Yet these two pointed sentences are overcome by a perfectly balanced following line, whose sentence spills over onto the next line and is followed by a short concluding question aimed at the voice of caution:

> But the juke-box inside me is playing a song
> That says something different. And when was it wrong?

There is a sense that some feelings can't be explained rationally, but must be experienced and acted upon, rather than repressed; the implication of the question is that the speaker's best decisions in the past have been made when paying attention to her instincts. Note the metaphor of the song being played by the juke-box for the feelings of love. It's quite a familiar image – perhaps the juke-box is the heart or the seat of the emotions, and the song represents the loving feelings at this particular time.

In the final stanza, the song inside her seems to be encouraging her to dance as she is 'tempted to skip' before being scolded by the inner voice of caution: '*You're a fool.*' But, by now, she has the confidence to silence this voice with an anapaest of three brisk monosyllables: 'I don't care'. The poem's final couplet closes the debate with the conclusion – delivered in punchy monosyllables in the penultimate line – that the heart is stronger than the head:

> The head does its best but the heart is the boss –
> I admit it before I am halfway across.

Michael Symmons Roberts (born 1963), 'To John Donne' (2004)

The speaker addresses John Donne and comments on the situation of him contemplating his mistress preparing for bed in the twenty-first century. As she removes her clothes, her body is already mapped out and known. Details of her are held in computers and understood by doctors. A path for the male's hands over his mistress' body has already been set, and while she lets his hands roam, she isn't really the one to give permission, since her body – like her lover's – has already been mapped out and patented. The speaker exhorts the lovers to trespass on their own bodies and reclaim them by whispering the numbers that make up their genetic codes.

Context

The poem was commissioned for an anthology of poetry exploring environmental issues – entitled *Wild Reckoning* (2004). Roberts worked with Sir John Sulston, the head of the team at Cambridge University who mapped the human genome (the complete set of genetic information encoded in a person's body). Sulston is an outspoken critic of those who want to patent parts of this information for commercial gain.

Taking it further ▶▶

The poem's epigraph expresses opposition to the idea of patenting a gene. Explain and comment on the language that Sulston uses and its effects.

Commentary Roberts' poem re-imagines Donne's famous 'Elegy 19: To His Mistress Going to Bed' being written in the twenty-first century. He reworks the language of conquest and possession – which Donne used to express the wonder at exploring the woman's body – to comment on love in the time of genetic patenting. The opening sentence offers a situation familiar to readers of Donne, with a woman preparing for bed with a man, but without the sense of sexual anticipation. The 'Now as your mistress strips for bed' does not lead to erotic thoughts, but the declaration that 'her body is already mapped,/its ancient names a cracked code.'

Roberts alludes to the excited exclamations of Donne, who in a memorable **metaphysical conceit** compared being with his mistress to discovering a new continent: 'O my America! My new found land!' Yet in the twenty-first-century poem the tone has become muted:

> That new found land is paced out,
> sized up, written down as hope
> or prophecy, probability or doubt.

The bodily descriptions are shadowed by the sense that she has already been possessed, not by an eager lover, but by corporations: 'laid bare' is not an arousing state of nakedness, but conveys the idea that her genetic code has been made plain: 'Her charts are held on laptops,/mastered by medics'. Note also how Donne's first person narration in heroic couplets and stately verse paragraphs have become tercets, whose half rhymes are appropriate to the dissatisfied tone of the third person commentary.

Donne's bold mixing of the loving and the religious has been debased by the language of science and medicine. No longer a 'mystic book' to be known and appreciated by the select few, the woman has her genetic code mapped out and her body is 'a textbook of disease'. A ghost of the active enjoyment that was palpable in Donne's poem is present in some of Roberts' wording; the man might have 'roving hands', but the right to touch or explore her body has been reserved by those who own her genetic code:

> … she's no landowner.
> By law, her breast's
>
> curve has a patent, so you know
> that bankers – tired of gold –
> have bought a piece of her and you.

Note how Roberts' third person speaker is able to cast a cold eye on the man and the woman: both have been conquered from within. The earlier metaphysical conceit of the woman as America is returned to after the midway point of the poem and the potential readings of Donne as a sexist or a colonist are rendered void as Roberts offers images for this new America: images ranging from the wide angle views of 'wilderness' and 'prairies/[that] have been carved up into real estate' to a close up of the sign warning the unauthorised to 'KEEP OUT/OUR DOGS EAT TRESPASSERS'.

Yet 'To John Donne' is much more than a polemic against the patenting of genetic information; it is a love poem. There is a shift in tone in the tenth stanza as the speaker moves closer to the couple, directly questioning them and suggesting that – on one level – the knowledge of their genetic codes doesn't really matter. The imagery and diction grow more conducive to love as 'at this fleet May dusk' they 'seek each other out'. The half rhyme that earlier seemed appropriate to a dissatisfying disconnection now sounds a softer note: the 'u' sound of 'dusk' finding a similarity in the 'ou' sound of 'out' and, until the final three lines, the stanzas become half-rhyming **triplets**.

The lovers in the poem are more equally balanced than those in Donne's, where the male speaker has been criticised as a sexist or a colonist. In many ways, Roberts' lovers are similar: 'her body's secret name is much/like' his. **Pastoral** imagery helps to extend the loving qualities as – in a new **metaphysical conceit** – the man's genetic make-up is compared to that of 'the crab apple and silver birch'. The imagery extends, as the couple are about to make love, to a beautiful description of natural harmony at twilight as the apple and birch

TASK

Take notes on both the subject matter and the poet's methods of Donne's 'Elegy XIX: To his Mistress Going to Bed'. Consider the extent to which you believe this to be a beautiful expression of love from a man to his loved one. Think about the methods used – especially the techniques such as metaphysical conceits.

... interweave with collar doves
and greenfinches, akin to grass
which drapes in blossom as the light dies.

The poem's final two stanzas comprise an imperative sentence that fades out. The speaker instructs the couple to reclaim their bodies through the physical expression of their love and – in a deft homage to Donne's mixing of the sacred and the profane – by whispering a litany which is comprised of the coordinates of one part of the human genome. It is, of course, a part that has already been patented.

CRITICAL VIEW

Joanna Luft writes:

> By turning the 'cracked code' into a litany, the lovers place it in the service of a love that, like 'Elegy 19,' combines the sacred and erotic. Moreover, as a public and participatory form of prayer, the litany counters the act of privatization. By chanting this particular sequence of patented genetic code, the lovers challenge the process whereby the corpus becomes the property of the corporation. The lovers also petition God for aid in this 'mass trespass,' an expression that contains a pun on the Christian 'Mass,' whose central Eucharistic words are 'This is my body.' The word 'trespass' ironically evokes the Lord's Prayer and its real, moral 'trespasses,' suggesting the absurdity of the charge that speaking about your own body is a violation of someone else's rights. By copying this DNA sequence into a public document, Roberts inaugurates the trespass he envisions.

(Joanna Luft, 'Roberts's 'To John Donne' and Donne's 'Elegy 19', *The Explicator*)

Carol Ann Duffy (born 1955), 'The Love Poem' (2005)

The speaker begins with: 'Till love exhausts itself, longs/for the sleep of words' and offers a range of fragments from famous love poems that comment on loved ones or yearn for them – from Shakespeare's 'my mistress' eyes' to Sir Walter Scott's 'one hour with thee'. The next stanza continues on a similar theme – 'Till love gives in and speaks/in the whisper of art' – and considers times when the lovers are together. They begin with the intense moment from the middle of Sir Thomas Wyatt's 'They Flee from Me' in which the woman asks the speaker, 'dear heart, how like you this?' and end with a quotation from Thomas Campion's poem, 'there is a garden in her face'. The final stanza begins 'Till love is all in *the* mind' and goes on to quote Donne – 'O my America!' – and the Bible – 'behold thou art fair' before going on to reflect on love being held in the mind and known by heart through poetry and concluding with a final thought that comes from Shelley: 'the desire of the moth/for the star.'

Taking it further
Having studied Donne's poem, compare it to Roberts' 'To John Donne'. How does your understanding of the former cast light on the latter?

Build critical skills
Read the quotation from Joanna Luft in the Critical view feature. What do you learn about Roberts' use of biblical language from this? Explain what she means by saying 'By copying this DNA sequence into a public document, Roberts inaugurates the trespass he envisions.'

Commentary 'The Love Poem' is a literary **collage** exploring both love and some of the ways in which it has been rendered in verse through the ages. Its title suggests universality — the whole genre of poetry as well as, perhaps, the love poem — that is, the definitive poem about love, which might sound like an immodest title, until we consider that its words are largely comprised of some of the most beautiful reflections on love from the best poets in the history of English literature.

Duffy writes in **free verse** with 12-line stanzas that contain spaced out lines, allowing the reader to ponder each use of another poet's words. None of the stanzas contain a main verb, so there is a kind of hovering feel to the poem as no thought is complete. The reader might be left wondering: what happens when love exhausts itself, gives in and speaks in the whisper of art, or when it is all in the mind? Perhaps the answers lie in the work of the other appropriated writers, or perhaps we are not meant to expect the logic of completed sentences when we are thinking so deeply about the many wonderful qualities of love.

Apart from quotations from other poets, 'The Love Poem' is full of references to writing: from the 'white sheet' that could as easily be on a desk as a bed in the first stanza to 'love's lips pursed to quotation marks/kissing a line' in the second and the 'pen/in the writer's hand' in the third. Indeed the poem might be read as being as much a love poem to poetry as to love itself. Consider the final stanza in which art is elevated to the level of religion.

> ## CRITICAL VIEW
>
> *Poetry, above all, is a series of intense moments — its power is not in narrative. I'm not dealing with facts, I'm dealing with emotion.*
>
> (Carol Ann Duffy, quoted in The Poetry Archive)
>
> To what extent is this borne out by your reading of 'The Love Poem'?

TASK

Read, or re-read, the poems that Duffy uses in 'The Love Poem'. Consider why you think each has been chosen and explain what aspect of love it might be seen to represent.

Here are some examples:

- 'let me count the ways' from 'How do I love thee' by Elizabeth Barret Browning
- 'come live/with me' from 'The Passionate Shepherd to His Love' by Christopher Marlowe
- 'look in thy heart/and write' from *Astrophil and Stella*: 'Sonnet 1' by Sir Philip Sidney
- 'behold thou art fair' from 'Song of Solomon 4:1' in *The King James Bible*.

Themes

Target your thinking

As you read this section, ask yourself the following questions:

- What subjects, or issues do the poems address; what ideas do they raise or explore? (**AO1**)
- Which themes do the poems and your comparative novel share? In what ways might you make thematic connections? (**AO4**)
- How might your appreciation of the poems' themes and concerns be shaped by your understanding of contexts? (**AO3**)
- In what ways might understanding more about themes open up alternative interpretations of the poems? (**AO1**)

Themes may be thought of as the ideas or concerns that the author addresses in the text: the topics or issues that the writer wants to explore. Thinking in terms of themes is a useful way to group your thoughts, and you may wish to subdivide a large theme into smaller sub-groups. A literary text, however, is not a simple, unilateral form of communication that seeks to transmit a straightforward message; readers, reviewers and critics often disagree on exactly what constitutes a text's main concerns. Even an author's views on this may not be fixed. Accordingly, themes are not discrete aspects, but are often connected; and part of the poet's skill is that he or she can often explore simultaneously several interlinked themes.

Throughout your study of your chosen section of the *Anthology*, be flexible enough to consider themes in different ways. Your secondary reading, for example, may lead you to consider a new theme or a theme in a new way. If you are studying A-level, your study of your comparative prose text may also help you see the issues of the poems in a new light. Concentrating on themes that recur throughout both your chosen prose text and section of the *Anthology* is also a good strategy for study. So, be willing to engage with new themes and new slants on themes you have already considered. This approach will serve you well as a preparation for the examination. After all, the question that you answer might specify an issue or concern of the poetry that you haven't considered, or hadn't considered in this way, before.

Unattainable love

Love that is beyond the reach of the lover holds a magnetic appeal for many writers. Whether it be unrequited love such as in Hardy's 'At an Inn' or the intense love and sadness that come from a parting, as in Burns' 'Ae Fond Kiss', or from just looking from afar and being dazzled as in Byron's 'She walks in beauty', love that fails somehow to gain full expression is a love that lingers long in the mind and is expressed with memorable intensity by the poet.

Unattainable love is also presented in Wyatt's 'Who so list to hount': there is the paradoxical feeling of knowing the pursuit is hopeless, yet feeling compelled to pursue the loved one. This poem might also be considered as an expression of love moving further out of reach as the speaker grows older: he is 'wearied', 'of them that furthest come behind' and 'fainting' as he follows his desire.

'La Belle Dame sans Merci' also depicts the consequences of pursuing an unattainable love. Love between a fairy's child and a human was never a long-term possibility and its consequences leave the knight 'haggard and woe-begone' and 'palely loitering' as he suffers the crushing lows of having tasted a powerful love yet knowing that he cannot experience it again. Keats' depiction of an unattainable love could have a range of thematic applications: it could be read as exploring the effects of experiencing sex with an adept or highly-desired lover, or with someone of a higher social class, who may toy with an 'ordinary' lover, but would never settle with someone of a lower social rank. In addition, the descriptions of the knight's withdrawal symptoms after his binge of love with the magical lover might suggest that the effects of such an unattainable love are like those associated with drug addiction.

A dissolute life is evoked more directly in 'Non Sum Qualis Eram Bonae sub Regno Cynarae' which is perhaps being led in consequence of the speaker's inability to sustain a wholesome love with Cynara. While the descriptions of the 'bought red mouth' and the 'warm heart' suggest that the speaker is involved in sexual relationships, it seems that – with the refrain telling of him being 'desolate and sick of an old passion' – real love is out of reach.

The unattainability of real love is also a concern of several of the writers in the post-1900 selection. Although the third person narrator in 'To John Donne' does suggest that the couple can make love in such a way as to reclaim their identities and their genetic codes from the corporations that patent them, the overriding feeling of the first two thirds of the poem is that love has been debased. The pleasures of the flesh celebrated by Donne have been undone and there is no longer any virgin territory to explore – both man and woman have already been mapped from within.

'Love and a Question' also depicts a scene of love – a husband and wife on their wedding night – but this quintessentially romantic situation is endangered by an outsider. Having the symbolic qualities of a parable without the message of one, Frost's poem explores the threats that love faces – even at its most secure moments – and makes the reader wonder the extent to which other duties impinge on love. From this poem, a perfect love does not seem to be attainable; on the couple's wedding night, the only images we have are of control (the heart encased and pinned) – and sexual frustration (the wife's rose red face by the open fire).

'For My Lover, Returning to His Wife' is another poem that explores the complex emotional difficulties of love. For the man, the complexities of adultery seem manageable; with a dutiful wife *and* an exciting mistress, he enjoys an excess of love. Yet, for his women, there are strains and there are sacrifices, and both, in their own ways, are presented as decorative items to enhance his life. Presenting adultery and its consequences from the point of view of the mistress, the poem's **free verse** outpouring of thoughts and feelings pays most attention to the woman being betrayed, rather than to the married man or to the mistress herself. The poem highlights gender inequality and the most obvious inference to draw is that in adultery the man is the winner, while both women lose. Consider how much emphasis is paid to what the women – particularly the wife – have given the man. The use of anaphora in the eighth stanza – 'I give you … /I give you' – underlines the inequality of the relationship between mistress and husband: she gives; he takes.

The pains of love

A poem that takes a different tack on some of the **pains of love** from a woman's perspective is 'I, being born a woman'. It explores the dichotomy between head and heart and explodes the myth that women always fall for the men they sleep with. The battle between physical needs and rational thoughts is explored in the tight form of a Petrarchan sonnet, leading to a resounding conclusion that asserts female power and punctures the male ego.

The **pains of love** are also evident as the poets explore parting, the event that occasions Anne Sexton's poem. 'Ae Fond Kiss' is heartfelt and lovelorn, but a poem that seems mannered and sweet in comparison to 'For My Lover, Returning to His Wife'. In Burns' poem the pain of parting is undoubtedly felt, but there might also be a kind of sentimental luxuriating in the feelings that it brings. At the other end of the scale is the parting in 'La Belle Dame sans Merci', which seems to have left the knight and his predecessors in a state of total ruin. The pains of parting – and, of course, of infidelity – are shown in 'The Scrutiny' and 'Absent from Thee', which respond in opposite ways. Lovelace shows a disdain for his lover, explaining in euphemisms his need to embark on new sexual adventures, while Rochester appears to show his compulsion for philandering as a weakness and one that will inevitably lead to mental torture and possibly the loss of his immortal soul.

Parting

Parting is explored differently in the post-1900 poems. In 'Wild Oats' the joke of the title is that the speaker did anything but sow wild oats; his pre-marital adventures were not like the riotous behaviour indulged in by poets like Dowson, Rochester or Lovelace, but boring cathedral visits, letter-writing and money wasted on a ring. The speaker seems indifferent at the parting and there is no description of the woman he left other than that she wore 'specs' and he 'could talk to' her. The parting of the couple in 'Timer' is an altogether more solemn

Taking it further

Compare the ways in which the consequences of infidelity are presented in 'For Her Lover Returning to His Wife' and in the comparative novel you are studying for Love through the Ages. If, for example, you are studying *Tess of the D'Urbervilles*, you might compare the presentation of female suffering and begin by looking back at Phase the Fifth. It deals with the consequences of Tess telling Angel about Alec and it is entitled 'The Woman Pays'.

and serious affair; the wit and comedy of Larkin is replaced by the sincerity of Harrison. The bond of the couple, like the ring that is its symbol, seems unbreakable and the reader respects the belief of the couple being together later, appreciating this in a broader way through the image of the ring in the centre of the timer: the grains of sand may fall from one end of the timer to the other, but in its centre is the circle through which they pass – a circle that represents eternity.

Marriage

Marriage is obviously a theme of 'Timer' and it is interesting to compare its representation to that of 'One Flesh'. The imagery of Jennings' poem is Christian, but there is little sense of the couple heading for an afterlife in which they will be united: their destination is 'Chastity'. Both poems explore marriage from the perspective of a grown-up child and it is interesting to consider how in one case the marriage seems so cold and separate, while in the other it outlasts the heat of cremation and the couple stay together beyond the grave. 'A quoi bon dire' also explores the idea that a couple can be together after death. Note how they are presented as sharing a common view of the world that is at odds with everyone else and how, in the light of love, ageing doesn't seem to take place. This is similar to the idea in 'One Flesh' where the daughter asks: 'Do they know they're old'; the daughter seems frustrated or upset at the couple's lack of recognition of their ageing, but in Mew's poem this aspect is presented through the eyes of the couple: their lack of care for ageing and death is not presented as a misconception but as a consolation and an amusing shared secret.

Another gloomy presentation of marriage – or at least a long-term relationship – is found in 'Talking in Bed'. As in Jennings' poem, the couple are depicted as being uncommunicative, but Larkin's perspective is disconcertingly both distant and close: he writes of the 'two people' and of the unsettled weather outside them, but he also writes 'none of this cares for us' as though writing from the point of view of one of the people in the bed. Thus, his concluding observations about a couple finding it increasingly difficult to be truthful or kind to one another seem to convey both a general truth and a bitter personal experience.

Perhaps the poem to explore marriage most overtly is Muldoon's 'Long Finish'. Celebratory and humorous, it uses allusions, puns, wit 'and then some' to offer a tribute to his wife after a decade of marriage. Even the ups and downs of married life take on a certain charm as they are presented humorously or paradoxically. Marriage is presented not as a slow train to sexlessness, but as a lively and satisfying state, where there is contentment and also gratified desire.

The joy of love

Poems like 'Timer' and 'A quoi bon dire' also explore the joys of love. Another poem that explores the same theme is 'Meeting Point'. In our busy lives we are often striving for goals and impatient to have what we want, but in this poem the couple savour the moment and we are invited to appreciate its beauty and to pause and recognise love's transformative powers which can turn the ordinary into the extraordinary. 'After the Lunch' dramatises the speaker's thoughts and feelings in response to a meal she has just shared. Ultimately gentle and joyful in its approach, the speaker moves towards the middle of Waterloo Bridge and she realises that she is in love. The battle that went on in her unconscious is explored in a much gentler manner than that in 'I, being born a woman'; the humorous battle leads to the heart being the victor (and the reader inwardly cheers).

The art of writing love poetry

Poems that address love in general also attest to its joys. Duffy's 'The Love Poem' is a medley of some of the most exquisite thoughts and feelings expressed on the topic, and the fragments chosen are not only beautiful, but joyful and celebratory. By exploring the joys of love, Duffy is also exploring the joys of writing about and reading about love. Shakespeare's 'Sonnet 116' also extols the virtues of love. While it does not shrink from alluding to its **pains** it is primarily concerned to show its enduring nature. Like Duffy's poem, Shakespeare's sonnet shows its love of words, and perhaps its ideas of love's permanence owe something to the poets who immortalise them in verse. In this way, several of the poems might be seen as being as much about poetry as they are about love. The self-referential aspects of poems like 'The Love Poem' (with its bricolage of quotations) and 'Sonnet 116' (with its **self-praising** couplet about its author's writing) are easy to see, but it might also be interesting to view some of the other love poems as being concerned with literary traditions as well as with love. For example, 'The Flea' or 'To His Coy Mistress' become different types of poem if we view them primarily as clever *carpe diem* poems written to please other men with their daring approaches to common poetic subjects.

Love and society's attitudes

In the eyes of many societies, while marriage is the ideal context in which sex should take place, there are spoken and unspoken rules that govern sexual behaviour out of wedlock. These **social concerns** are explored by many of the poems. At one end is 'At an Inn' which, it could be argued, explores a love that could go no further owing to the harsh stance of Victorian society on adultery – a stance that has been internalised by the female character and in turn has led to a cooling in the relationship, which had already gone beyond the bounds of what would have been considered respectable. At the other is 'The Garden of Love', where sexual pleasure seems to have been prohibited by the Church. We never have the 'joys and desires', or what is forbidden by the words 'Thou Shalt Not' spelled out for us, but we gain the impression that whatever Blake or his contemporaries want to do, it is prohibited. The 'binding with briars' compounds the prohibition with a sense of torture. Society's attitudes are mocked in 'The Ruined Maid': a serious subject is treated in a humorous manner, with the result that we see the foolishness of adhering to certain social rules. In this topsy-turvy world the fallen woman is the one who has gone up in the world, leaving her countrywoman friend in a state of shock and envy.

TASK

As you study your chosen comparative novel, think about – and make notes on – themes, ideas and issues in which the writer is interested. Also think about any important symbols or motifs. Note different ways in which you could connect these themes, symbols and motifs to the poems from the *Anthology*. The greater your understanding of both of these texts, the easier it is going to be to make connections. So, make sure you look back at your comparative novel after you have studied the *Anthology* and vice versa.

Social pressures are felt every bit as harshly in the post-1900 poems. From the effects of war that kill off lovers, leaving widows and grieving girlfriends who had no part in the conflict, to the cruel treatment of a young woman who has defied the rules of her community and been sleeping with the enemy in 'Punishment'. This poem not only explores sympathy for the victim, it also interrogates the feelings of the bystanders in her community. Heaney explores the guilt of the many that lies in the wake of the violence perpetrated by the few and makes his readers confront their consciences and question the extent to which doing nothing is an active act of violence.

Other **themes** and issues that arise from the *Anthology* include, but are not limited to:

- strong feelings associated with love – from euphoria to selfishness and jealousy
- adultery and infidelity
- wooing
- sexuality
- time and its effects on love.

Taking it further ▶

Using the list of themes above and those in the main body of this section, work through each of the poems in your section of the *Anthology* making notes on each of the themes that it explores. You might like to make a concept map for each poem's themes, or to make one on a page large enough for you to include all of the poems' titles and to trace thematic connections between them. After you have done this, you could devise a labelling system. For example, you might use 'P' for parting, 'D' for death, 'A' for adultery and so on. Labelling your contents page so that the poem titles are followed by your symbols for themes is an effective way to recall themes and to see thematic connections quickly. Remember – be open to seeing new themes as your studies progress, and always be flexible enough to consider themes in various ways.

TASK

Invent a range of different ways of expressing the same theme and think of different subthemes within a single theme. For example, your synonyms for **Parting** might include leaving, farewells, goodbyes, moving on, separations and so on; your subthemes might include tearful goodbyes, mutual parting, being rejected, forced parting (through war, parental opposition, societal rules, etc). If you carry out tasks like these, you will find it much easier to be flexible in an exam situation, where the examiner chooses the theme or topic. In this situation a strong student is confident in considering the exact words that the question uses and can engage fully with them at the planning stage and throughout the answer.

The poets' methods

Target your thinking

As you read this section, ask yourself the following questions:

- Consider the different methods that the poets use in the *Anthology*: which are the most important to each poet, and how are they used to shape meaning and to create effects? (**AO2**)
- As you consider methods and meaning, note uses of literary terms; how can you use literary terminology to help you to articulate your responses with more precision and concision? (**AO1**)
- How might your understanding of the methods the poets use help you to make connections with your comparative novel? (**AO4**)
- In what ways can different close readings lead to alternative interpretations? (**AO5**)

Form and genre

Commenting on genres and **subgenres** is a part of responding to form. For example, it is helpful to be able to apply an understanding of the conventions of the **sonnet**. There are several sonnets in the *Anthology*: from 'Who so list to hount' by Wyatt (who helped develop this genre in English) to those by contemporary writers such as Harrison, whose 'Timer' stretches the boundaries of the **Meredithian sonnet**, opening up its stanzaic form to produce a text that has both the freedom to allow the narrative to unfold in a seemingly natural manner, but also the discipline and craft to contain powerful thoughts, symbols and feelings within a strict poetic form.

Some poems, such as 'Ae Fond Kiss', 'Absent from Thee' and 'The Scrutiny' were written as **songs**, and it is worth considering the influence of this form on these texts. *The New Princeton Encyclopedia of Poetry and Poetics* explains that song is a 'term used broadly to refer to verbal utterance that is musically expressive of emotion' and that as well as a piece of verse to be set to music, the term can apply to 'any poem focusing on the arousal of emotion'.

Many of the poems in the *Anthology* can be categorised into the genre of the **lyric** – a relatively short, non-narrative poem that expresses the mood or thoughts and feelings of the speaker. For example, 'Non Sum Qualis Eram Bonae sub Regno Cynarae' and 'She Walks in Beauty' from the pre-1900 section, as well as 'Meeting Point' and 'A Quoi Bon Dire' from the post-1900 section are lyric poems. Lyric poems are often associated with musicality and are usually well-made poems in which each of the parts contributes to the overall harmony;

TASK

Discover more about the sonnet through research and further reading. For example, you might read the engaging and informative introduction to Don Patterson's *101 Sonnets* or visit a comprehensive and authoritative site all about the sonnets of Shakespeare at: www.shakespeares-sonnets.com/intro.php

TASK

Conduct internet searches for the songs in the pre-1900 section of the *Anthology*, for videos and sites that have musical versions of the texts. As a starting point, why not visit http://www.bbc.co.uk/arts/robertburns/works/ae_fond_kiss

TASK

Discover more about the lyric by using glossaries of literary terms and websites such as https://web.cn.edu/kwheeler/lit_terms_L.html

How does knowing more about the genre of lyric poetry help you to appreciate the lyric poems in the part of the *Anthology* that you are studying?

often passionate, they often communicate powerful emotions and deal with personal subject matter. While many glossaries of literary terms classify several types of poem – including song, sonnet and elegy – as subgenres of the lyric, the term lyric is a useful way to categorise poems that express personal emotion, but whose genre you don't recognise and which could neither be considered dramatic nor narrative poetry.

Taking it further ▷

'Lyric' comes from the Greek (*lyra*) – a musical instrument – and the term has broadened in meaning to denote the words of songs. In 2008 an examination at the University of Cambridge instructed English students to compare a lyric poem by Sir Walter Raleigh with the lyrics of one or two of the songs printed in the examination paper. Most of these songs were by well-known poets from throughout the ages.

The exam was widely discussed in the press because one of the choices was not by a literary author, but 'Love is a Losing Game' by the singer and songwriter, Amy Winehouse. Find out more about this by conducting a web search.

What do you think can be gained by studying a genre and comparing different texts within that genre? To what extent do you think that lyrics by Winehouse could be worthy of academic study?

Narrative poems are those that recount stories – which have a clear sequence of events and which usually involve defined characters. Such poems in the *Anthology* include 'At an Inn' and 'La Belle Dame sans Merci' from the pre-1900 section and 'Wild Oats' from the post-1900 section. Note that poems are not always exclusively narrative; for example, '*Vergissmeinnicht*' contains both narrative and lyric elements.

When you identify a narrative element in a poem it is often helpful to think about the functions of any characters in the story, the significance of the events chosen and the way in which they are sequenced. For example, you might ask yourself some of the following questions: in what ways might elements in the narrative foreshadow later events, build tension or deliver surprises; how does the narrative use contrasts or repetition; is there a climax, a resolution or a concluding section that expands on the story's significance; is there a cyclical effect, or does the narrative progress in a linear fashion?

Sometimes you can explore the genre of a narrative in a poem and the ways in which the poet plays with the reader's expectations of a genre. For example, the opening of 'La Belle Dame sans Merci' might be read as a Romance, but when we realise that the character whom we might have considered as the heroine (La Belle Dame) shifts into the villain (or a *femme fatale* – a beautiful but deadly woman), we might read this poem as a **Gothic** narrative, which casts many of the details that we read earlier in a sinister light.

The poems in the post-1900 section of the *Anthology* range widely in genre, from the expressive **free verse** of poems like 'For My Lover, Returning to his Wife' to the intricate use of the **ballade** in 'Long Finish'.

Considering **stanzaic form** and how this changes within a poem can also be a fruitful course of study. Note how, for instance, the **tercets** of Larkin's 'Talking in Bed' seem to suit the subject matter of the poem in which a couple are unable to communicate. The first and third lines of the first three stanzas contain half rhyme – they almost rhyme but not quite. For example:

> Talking in bed ought to be **easiest**,
> Lying together goes back so far,
> An emblem of two people being **honest**.

This lends a sense of dissatisfaction to the poem, which is fitting for one about people in an intimate setting, but who aren't intimate, who 'ought to' find it easiest to speak openly when in bed together, but don't. End rhyme also draws attention to the last rhyming word – in this case 'honest'. While it seems that they are in a situation in which they should be honest, they are not. Their situation is emblematic of 'two people being honest', but the subtext is clear: they are not.

The poem picks up on the idea of honesty again in the final **tercet**. But look how the stanzaic form has shifted from tercets to a **triplet** (a three-line stanza in which every line rhymes). After a line of the poem's typical iambic pentameter – 'It becomes still more difficult to find' – the poem concludes with two shorter lines. The first is short and somewhat faltering – 'Words at once true and kind' – and the last is clear and iambic – 'Or not untrue and not unkind'. Note how the rhymes have changed from half rhymes to full rhymes. A full rhyme – especially after a succession of half rhymes – might be expected to sound a note of conclusion and certainty. This one does, but what it is certain about is the difficulties in a relationship: how difficult it is not just to communicate, but to say something kind or honest. Even the look of the stanza on the page reinforces its sense of the difficulties in a couple's relationship. The last two lines look like a couplet, but they're not: an irregular line of six syllables doesn't match a line of iambic tetrameter, and the final rhyming sound at first seems to be unique to the final stanza's last two lines, but it's not: it was already heard in the line above.

Sound effects

While many of the comments on poetic methods above draw your attention to ways in which effects are created through form, structure and language, there are also other effects that are significant particularly to the emotional resonance of the poems that comes from their musicality. This is particularly evident in the lyric poems and in the songs. For example, if you listen to the recording of 'Ae Fond Kiss' on the BBC site you can appreciate even more fully the ways in which the heavy double rhymes (when two syllables rather than one rhyme, such as

TASK

If you can place a poem in a genre or poetic form, it is always worth finding out more about that form. Consider the extent to which the form or genre suits the speaker and/or the subject matter of the poem. Think about any changes to the conventions of the form/genre; what has the poet gained by any adaptations made?

Build critical skills

Use a good guide to literary terms to discover more about poetic forms. There are also several useful glossaries online. The following page includes helpful entries on ballad and ballade: https://web.cn.edu/kwheeler/lit_terms_B.html

in 'sever' and 'for**ever**') suit being accompanied by music and how the whole poem, with its many repetitions and its open avowals of love, suits the genre of song. This is something that needs to be experienced: when you hear the words sung there is an impact that cannot be fully appreciated simply through study.

CRITICAL VIEW

Having listened to the song being sung, and using examples from the text, explain what Pauline Gray means by the following assessment:

Burns' use of the song to express his distress at the finality of the pair's relationship is both dramatic and emotive. 'Ae Fond Kiss' conveys sincere, powerful notions of love, and yet a sense of deep despair and hopelessness is ever present.

(www.bbc.co.uk/arts/robertburns/works/ae_fond_kiss)

Similarly, Byron's 'She Walks in Beauty' gains from being considered in terms of its sound. The strong regularity of the iambic tetrameter makes the poem suitable for setting to music. The repetition and the poem's simplicity also help; as the poem rhymes *ababab cdcdcd efefef*, there are only six rhyming sounds in the entire poem. Poetic effects rarely work in isolation, so think about how a poem's musicality enhances its ideas. Harmony is a major idea, so you might like to consider the ways in which rhyme links opposites by sound, thus reinforcing the idea of a beauty that unites contrary elements, making them harmonise: for instance, the poem's first rhyming word 'night' has full rhymes with two words that are its opposites – 'bright' and 'light'.

CRITICAL VIEW

Frye disparages Bryon's lyric poetry further by stating that it 'contains nothing that "modern" critics look for: no texture, no ambiguities, no intellectualized ironies, no intensity, no vividness of phrasing, the words and images being vague to the point of abstraction'.
To what extent do you feel Frye's criticisms are applicable to 'She Walks in Beauty'?

Context

'She Walks in Beauty' appeared in an 1815 collection entitled *Hebrew Melodies*, the poems from which were to be set to versions of traditional Jewish tunes. Critics often cite the musicality of Byron's lyrics as their major strength. Not all critics praise Hebrew Melodies. Northrope Frye said the lyrics have 'flat conventional diction appropriate to poems that depend partly on another art for their sound' (Salusinszky (ed.), 2005).

The sound of some of the poems in the post-1900 section is also integral to their impact. For example, '*Vergissmeinnicht*' and 'Timer' are both elegiac lyric poems, which move readers through the sincerity of the emotions they convey, not only through the stories they tell but also through the musical language they use. Like the poem by Byron, neither uses complex diction, but communicates in a simple, sincere but powerful way. Consider, for example, the way in which 'Timer' uses simple **cross-rhyme** throughout, adding an unobtrusive poetic dimension to the narrative comprised of ordinary diction. It also links ideas and draws attention to contrasts. For example, the idea of cremation is suggested by 'urn' and 'burn', but we might also note the contrasts between the unremarkable '**standard** urn' and the magical-sounding wedding ring which '**wouldn't** burn'. The importance of the ring is also reinforced through sound elsewhere in the poem. In the second stanza internal rhyme reinforces its symbolic purpose for the father: this 'eternity' is his 'surety' that he and his wife will be united in the afterlife. In the single line of the penultimate stanza, a concentration of 'm' sounds suggest that the ring is humming with power as it sits 'on my warm palm now'. And, in the three lines of the final stanza, when Harrison unites the ring symbol with that of the timer, sibilance suggests the slippage of the ashes through the central ring-like part of the egg timer as well as the hushed wonder of the speaker:

> I feel your ashes, head, arms, breasts, womb, legs,
> sift through its circle slowly, like that thing
> you used to let me watch to time the eggs.

If you are able to perform the poems yourself, or listen to recordings of actors or the poets themselves reading aloud, you can often appreciate their aural qualities even further. For example, you might wish to consider the rhythmic qualities and the uses of repetition, refrain, alliteration and varied tone in 'Non Sum Qualis Eram Bonae sub Regno Cynarae'. You can find some great recordings of readings of the poem using an internet search. An excellent one by Richard Burton is available on YouTube.

You can take a similar approach to 'For My Lover, Returning to His Wife'. Consider the ebb and flow of emotion in the poem and the places where the pace picks up, where the tone changes and how repetition creates effects. Have a look on YouTube at a recording of Anne Sexton reading the poem.

Advice on analysing poetic methods

While this section has necessarily focused on particular poetic methods, remember that it is often most impressive when you comment on how several effects work together to create meaning and effects. Rather than simply focusing on features that are obvious, select those that are most significant to the poem overall and those most relevant to the question you are answering. Avoid commenting on isolated details without a sense of their wider meaning; you can keep a strong sense of the meaning of details by reading whole clauses and whole sentences. For example, if you were exploring the use of **personification** in 'At an Inn' a superficial reading might say that the couple were in love for a long time since 'Love lingered'; a more considered reading would recognise what came before and after the two isolated words and realise that their time at the inn was loveless:

> The kiss their zeal foretold
> And now deemed come,
> Came not: within his hold
> Love lingered numb.

Beware of simply naming features, and keep meaning to the fore as you write. For example, if you comment on a metaphor or a simile, think about what is being compared to what, what the two have in common and how the comparison changes the reader's perception.

Taking it further ▶▷

Find out more about the ways in which metaphor and simile work by consulting glossaries of literary terms, where you should be able to find out more about the terms, such as tenor (the subject the metaphor describes) and vehicle (the metaphorical item to which the tenor is compared). These terms were coined by the critic I.A. Richards to help explore such figurative language with precision. The following site is a good starting point: www.britannica.com/art/tenor-literature

Contexts

Target your thinking

As you read this section, ask yourself the following questions:

- How does contextual material help you to deepen your understanding of the poems? (**AO1**)
- In what ways can you apply contextual readings or critical approaches to the poems? (**AO3**)
- How does contextual understanding help you to make connections to your comparative novel? (**AO4**)
- In what ways might your understanding of contexts lead you to consider alternative interpretations? (**AO5**)

Contextual meanings are not those found within the text, but those that exist around it. They might, for example, arise from the details of an author's life or the times in which he or she lived, or be related to literary movements or genres that are relevant to their writing. A further type of context is a critical perspective that a reader might adopt as they study the text – for example, a Marxist or a psychoanalytical approach.

Given that the *Anthology* is comprised of a range of different poems, there are numerous ways in which contextual readings can be applied. Accordingly, this section cannot aim to be comprehensive in its treatment of context, but offers a selection of ways in which you might use contexts to illuminate the poems. Remember that, as well as this separate section, there are a variety of context features throughout the guide as a whole.

Biographical contexts

It is often worth exploring the biographies of each of the writers to discover ways in which their lives might cast light on their work. While it is unhelpful to make an easy equivalence between poet and speaker, in some cases there are events that inspire poems. For example, it is interesting to consider Sir Henry Wyatt's biography and reflect on the extent to which his relationship with Anne Boleyn is dramatised in the poem. Anne was said to have had a strong sexual magnetism that drew many men to her, and Sir Thomas Wyatt, a handsome, tall and accomplished man of the Court, was no exception. There are several stories of dalliances between the two, but it is uncertain whether Wyatt was having sexual relations with Anne while she was Queen, or at any other time. What is certain is that Wyatt was imprisoned – for what is thought to be suspected adultery against the King – at the time of Anne's downfall.

Taking it further ▶

Visit the website of the Robert Burns Birthplace Museum and view some of the letters he wrote to Agnes McLehose. Consider how much your understanding of this relationship can enhance your appreciation of the song 'Ae Fond Kiss'.

http://burnsmuseum.org.uk/collections/object_detail/3.6363

A relationship outside of wedlock of a less dangerous sort was conducted between Robert Burns and Mrs Agnes McLehose – the 'Nancy' of 'Ae Fond Kiss'. While Burns is sometimes portrayed as a ploughman poet, a lothario or a drunk, he was a much more sophisticated and complex figure than such simplifications suggest. His friendship with McLehose seems to have been a courtly, genteel and literary affair that was conducted largely through letters in which they adopted the pastoral pen-names 'Sylvander' and 'Clarinda'. While flirtation, flattery and fine feelings abound in their correspondence, it is interesting to consider those occasions on which Burns' feelings of friendship heat to the point where they boil over into desire – as he wrote to 'Clarinda', early in their relationship:

> *I believe there is no holding converse or carrying on correspondence, with an amiable woman, much less a <u>gloriously amiable</u>, <u>fine woman</u>, without some mixture of that delicious Passion, whose most devoted Slave I have more than once had the honor of being…*

(Extract of a letter from Robert Burns to Mrs Agnes McLehose, dated 28 December 1787, Robert Burns Birthplace Museum – note that the underlining is Burns' own)

Hardy's relationship with Florence Henniker is worth thinking about when studying 'At an Inn', particularly when considering the extent to which events in the poem differ from what we know of real life. It could be argued that what is presented as a dramatic failure of the light of love to shine on the couple, who would later regret this missed opportunity bitterly, is actually a transmutation of a man's one-sided and calculating desire for a woman who was happy to flirt, but ultimately only ever wanted to be friends.

Knowing about the biography of John Donne is helpful when considering both his work and the ways in which it was written and first received. While eventually converting to the Church of England, Donne's religious ideas were shaped by Roman Catholicism; his mother, his father and two stepfathers all practised this faith at a time when it was outlawed in England.

Some also suggest secret Catholicism was the reason for Donne leaving Oxford University without taking a degree, as to take one would have required an oath of loyalty to the Church of England. Whatever the exact details of his life, most regard Roman Catholicism as being a preeminent influence on his work: in the words of Professor Peter McCullough, the imagery of Roman Catholicism 'saturates his poetry, both secular and religious'.

By the age of 20 Donne was studying at the Inns of Court in London. As well as being a place to study the law, this was a dynamic and exciting place to live and be young. Intelligence was prized and cleverness and wit were sharpened and displayed to those who might offer patronage or jobs at the Royal Court. It was here in his early twenties where most of Donne's famous poetry was written: not for publication, but to be circulated privately to an exclusive audience of witty male friends. Think about this audience and the poem's use of Roman Catholic imagery and symbolism as you study 'The Flea'.

Knowing more about the personal experiences of the writers can sharpen your appreciation, especially when you know that the material is autobiographical, as is the case with touching poems like '*Vergissmeinnicht*' and 'Timer'. Yet there are other occasions when it is misleading to assume autobiography plays too large a part in poetic creation. Larkin's 'Wild Oats' is a good example. The curmudgeonly speaker who enumerates the 'four hundred letters', 'ten guinea ring' and seven years wasted in courting the 'friend in specs', while secretly admiring the sexy photos of 'bosomy rose with fur gloves on' doesn't seem too far away from the Larkin who joked to male friends: 'I don't want to take a girl out and spend circa £5 when I can toss myself off in five minutes, free, and have the rest of the evening for myself.' (Quoted in *The Times Literary Supplement* on 12 November 2014.)

Yet this is only one side of the Larkin persona and doesn't capture the complexity of the poet's relationship with Ruth Bowman, the woman who inspired the fiancée in 'Wild Oats', or his shyness around women – something which is glimpsed in vulnerable moments of the poem such as 'She was trying/Both times (so I thought) not to laugh'.

By contrast, biography holds a different status in poets who deliberately use their lives as material. Anne Sexton began writing as a kind of therapy and her work is often categorised as falling into the **subgenre** of **confessional poetry**. While the poem is a well-wrought artistic creation that can be appreciated in its own right, many read 'For my Lover, Returning to his Wife' as a raw and direct response to an event in Sexton's life – the poet being left by her psychiatrist, Dr Ollie Zweizung, with whom she had been having an extra-marital affair. It has been pointed out that the poem even recycles some of the imagery that the doctor used in love poems to his patient. Unlike the relatively controlled poem, the response to the end of the affair took on much more destructive proportions, with Sexton taking an overdose and being hospitalised for 48 hours; later in an act of self-destructiveness on her birthday she fell down the stairs, injuring herself so badly that she would always thereafter walk with a limp. In view of the complex ways in which life and art intersect in Sexton's poetry some critics believe that traditional literary criticism is an inappropriate response to her work. In the words of J.D. McClatchy:

> *Anne Sexton's poems so obviously come out of deep, painful sections of the author's life that one's literary opinions scarcely seem to matter; one feels tempted to drop them furtively in the ashcan in the face of so much naked suffering.*

(McClatchy, 1978)

Of course, we could equally consider Sexton's work from a more historicist slant. It could be argued that 'For My Lover, Returning to his Wife' should be read as an expression of love in the swinging sixties. But, rather than showing the joys

Taking it further ▶

Read 'For My Lover, Returning to his Wife' from a feminist perspective. Draw a triangle with each of the characters at one point: the husband, the wife and the lover (the speaker). Write out the descriptions of each character, then make a list of all of the things — physical and emotional — that each gains from the relationship. Which character has the most power in the relationship, and how does this power affect the others?

Taking it further ▶

Discover more about Millay's life and consider how this knowledge might develop your response to her poem. Reviews of biographies are good places to start. For example, one in the *New York Times* from 2001 heralds her not only as a poet and a 'free spirit' who was the 'romantic rebel of the Jazz Age' but also as 'a rock star, the Madonna of her time'. You can search for this review online by visiting the New York Times website.

of free love, it expresses its pains. Furthermore, the division of pleasures and pains seem to be along strict gender lines: the man gets the pleasure (an exciting mistress and a devoted wife), while the women get the pains (a straying husband, or a man leaving you in a state of loneliness and emotional turmoil). Such a line of thought could lead you to question the very nature of sexual freedom — at least for the suburban middle classes.

Historical and biographical contexts are also helpful when considering another poet associated with the earlier age of sexual freedom, the Jazz Age (the late 1910s and the 1920s); Edna St Vincent Millay is sometimes celebrated as its poetic embodiment. Not only were the 1920s a time of economic prosperity, they also enabled women to have greater levels of liberation. In 1920 in America, women gained the vote and the 'flapper' style became fashionable, with women wearing bobbed hair, short dresses and make-up. Attitudes changed too, with the questioning of the previous **patriarchal** assumptions that cast the man as the provider and the woman in the supporting role, and many women experimented for the first time with free love and illegal alcohol and drugs. While the true flapper lifestyle was perhaps only completely available to a certain set of women, the flapper became a widely reported and influential phenomenon. Millay certainly embodied many of its values. She drank and lived hedonistically, famously burning the candle at both ends. Even when married she continued to have affairs, which her devoted husband seemed to accept; and, at home, she neither cooked, shopped nor cleaned.

Build critical skills

In what ways do you think the following quotation from 'First Fig', a poem by Edna St Vincent Millay, might cast light on her lifestyle and attitudes and those of young fashionable women of the 1920s?

> *My candle burns at both ends;*
> *It will not last the night;*
> *But ah, my foes, and oh, my friends —*
> *It gives a lovely light!*

Biographical material can also be interesting when we consider how a writer's life fits into wider historical and political concerns. Seamus Heaney's early collections are notable for being rooted in the soil of his native land, with life and work in rural County Derry/Londonderry giving rise to much of the subject matter and the settings for these poems. Even those dealing with the everyday tensions between Catholics and Protestants, such as 'The Other Side', have their roots in real-life experience. While a Catholic Nationalist, Heaney had avoided overt political engagement and refused to put his poetry to the service of the Nationalist cause. Tensions, however, rose during the mid-1970s, when the violence in Northern

Ireland escalated to its worst point; but, rather than use his poetry to make the kind of direct statements about the conflict that he had hitherto avoided, Heaney sought to explore the issues indirectly. In an essay entitled 'Feeling into Words' he expresses the need to give voice to complexities of feeling and to do so in ways that are honest and true: to 'encompass the perspectives of a humane reason and at the same time to grant the religious intensity of the violence its deplorable authenticity and complexity'. Rather than make direct statements in his poetry, Heaney sought to do more: to find 'images and symbols adequate to our predicament'. (Heaney: *Preoccupations*, 1984)

There is a strong sense that by the time he was writing the collection *North* (1975) he had found such symbols and images. Beginning as a meditation on the hanged body of an Iron Age adulteress, 'Punishment' is able to explore not only an ugly sectarian act of punishment within the Catholic community, but also to confront the complex and atavistic (primitive and ancestral), feelings that such acts engender. This confrontation produces much more than a cry of outrage at how such things as tarring and feathering can be allowed in a civilised society. It lays bare the ugly feelings that rise up even within the moderates in Northern Irish society, as Heaney articulates unpleasant truths and places them in wider contexts of tribal customs and religious beliefs.

Literary contexts

Understanding different literary periods, movements and genres enables you not only to appreciate other ways in which the poems might be read but also to make connections between them and other texts.

Genre

Whether we realise it or not, we read texts with a sense of the other texts we have read; our past reading sets up expectations of what we read in the present. This dynamic means that we often feel pleasure when our expectations are fulfilled. For example, when reading a detective story, we expect there to be a crime and there to be an eccentric, but highly intelligent, detective; we also expect that by the end of the story he or she will have solved the crime, with the criminal's identity and the solution to trapping him or her coming to us as something of a surprise. Too much conformity to generic conventions, however, can lead to predictability and a diminishing of the reader's pleasure. Accordingly, writers often bend generic rules and their work entertains through a mixture of pleasure at conforming to some conventions and surprise at breaking others.

Pastoral

From *pastor*, the Latin for 'shepherd', the **pastoral** may be thought of as the literary genre that features idealised representations of the countryside, with examples from early modern literature often featuring depictions of shepherds and shepherdesses enjoying love and leisure in the open air. It is a style that often reflects the yearnings of sophisticated city dwellers for a harmonious, simple country life they have never known – a life that never really existed. As the eighteenth-century poet Alexander Pope wrote of how poets should make their work delight the reader:

> *We must therefore use some illusion to render a Pastoral delightful and this consists in exposing the best side only of a shepherd's life and concealing its miseries.*

(Pope in Croker (ed.), 1871)

There is a hint of the pastoral in some of the post-1900 poems, such as 'A Quoi Bon Dire' and 'To John Donne'. Both use pastoral imagery to help evoke a new mood in their concluding stanzas. Mew's poem imagines the ageing speaker and her dead husband reunited 'one fine morning in a sunny lane' and exchanging the looks and gestures of a young couple. Roberts uses imagery of trees, grass and blossom as a backdrop to the couple whom he encourages to reclaim their bodies. In both cases, such language lends the poem a sense of hope as well as idealism.

Gothic

This genre, associated with the author's desire to horrify, terrify or thrill includes typical settings such as ruined castles, monasteries, graveyards and dungeons; typical **Gothic** villains include overreaching scientists, corrupt priests and supernatural beings. Imperilled young women are typical victims, and, as well as actual events that shock, nightmares or other extreme states of mind are often depicted.

'The Garden of Love' plays with both pastoral and Gothic conventions, with the idyllic nature of the garden as it was when the speaker was a boy being evoked through pastoral imagery and the horror of what it turned into being presented in Gothic features. The final stanza presents the terror of the chilling transformation, where 'tombstones' and sinister-looking 'priests in black gowns' are administering a deep-rooted mental torture, and where 'joys and desires' are being bound with briars.

While the word 'Gothic' in *'Vergissmeinnicht'* refers primarily to the style of Steffi's writing on the photograph she gave to her sweetheart, the German gunner, there is a strong sense in this poem that, in war, love turns to horror. Douglas uses a disturbing supernatural simile when he writes of the German shell, which hit the speaker's tank 'like the entry of a demon', and the imagery surrounding the aftermath of the battle, when the speaker imagines a nightmarish meeting between the weeping Steffi and the body of her dead lover, is as horrific as something from a Gothic novel:

> But she would weep to see today
> How on his skin the swart flies move;
> The dust upon the paper eye
> And the burst stomach like a cave.

While such imagery is used in 'Vergissmeinnicht' to shock the reader with the horror of war and to provide a contrast to the more lyrical language of the last stanza, in 'To His Coy Mistress' Gothic imagery is seemingly used by the speaker to strike fear into the heart of the mistress and persuade her to be more responsive to his overtures. The language of the bedchamber has crumbled into the language of the graveyard as Marvell's speaker offers a bleak vision of the fate that awaits the addressee if she fails to accept his advances. In a 'marble vault' she will no longer hear the reverberations of his poetry and 'Worms shall try/That long preserv'd Virginity'. Likewise, her 'quaint honour' will turn to 'dust', like his lustful feelings which will then be no more than 'ashes'. The use of Gothic imagery might be seen to portray the wasting of youthful sexuality as a horrific perversion. Subtextual meanings also add to the sense of horror and disgust. For example, the graveworms that try her virginity might be seen as a hideous perversion of phallic imagery.

When the features of one genre are blended with another, interesting and unusual effects can ensue, as you will know if you have seen, for example, a film that mixes elements of comedy and horror. 'La Belle Dame sans Merci' with its dialogue between knights leads the reader to expect a chivalric tale, but the symbolic use of nature in details, such as the harvest being over and the lily on the knight's brow, lends the narrative an undertone of disquiet. With the introduction of the story of meeting the 'lady in the meads' there is a shift in mood. His story begins on a hopeful note and there is something pleasantly pastoral about his meeting a beautiful woman in a meadow and adorning her with flowers. The reader who is familiar with the pastoral genre might expect the story to develop into a tale of love and idleness, but the idea of the beautiful woman being 'a fairy's child' begins to show its influence as the leisurely luxury of the lovers' time together is undermined by elements of the supernatural, such as the 'language strange' and the lady's 'wild wild eyes'. By the time he has fallen asleep, the knight's tale has crossed over completely to the Gothic genre as he suffers from a tortuous nightmare featuring deathly kings and princes who warn him of the spell under which he has fallen and which will leave him in discontent for the rest of his life.

Metaphysical poetry

Just as genres develop in response to changing times and the needs of new audiences, so too new styles of verse emerge in response to older ones. While Shakespeare was mocking the conventions of Petrarchan verse (traditional love poetry that, among other features, lavishes praise on the loved one, comparing her to the beauties of nature and adopting a lovestruck mood) from within the sonnet genre, others were developing completely new styles. John Donne was prominent amongst a group of writers who did just that. Their poetry is dramatic and engaging, characterised by complex arguments and elaborate, arresting comparisons that bring together elements in ways that might at first seem highly unlikely, but which upon closer scrutiny are seen to be clever, witty and, ultimately, true.

The overtly intellectual qualities of such poetry were gently mocked by later poets including John Dryden, in 1672, when he criticised the way in which Donne's work 'affects the metaphysics, not only in his satires, but in his amorous verses, where nature only should reign; and [he] perplexes the minds of the fair sex with nice speculations of philosophy, when he should engage their hearts'. The term 'metaphysical poets' was popularised by Samuel Johnson who implied that there was something forced and unsatisfactory about their wit, where 'the most heterogeneous ideas are yoked by violence together'. Many readers, however, have come to appreciate the virtues of metaphysical poetry, which can be seen as humorous as well as intellectual, loving as well as logical. 'The Flea' is a good example. Its central conceit – where the flea that has sucked the blood of both lovers comes to be an embodiment of their love and represents a kind of sexual union between them – is both clever and comical. On one level, it might be read as an intellectual game, played more to win the admiration of the male friends who made up the coterie of wits who shared each other's poetry while studying at the Inns of Court than the heart of any real female; on another, it might be read as a lyric in which the speaker, if not the poet, might be using – rather than the flattering clichés of conventional Elizabethan verse – the full resources of his wit and intelligence in a daring and direct attempt at seduction.

There is a harder edge to Marvell's verse in 'To His Coy Mistress' where the speaker presents the addressee with the stark choice of using her young and beautiful body to make love with him or being ravished by time and rotting in her grave as an unenjoyed virgin. Like Donne's work, most of Marvell's was not published in his lifetime, but circulated in manuscript form, and it could be argued that poems such as 'To His Coy Mistress' were written to entertain and to display his intellect to male friends. Just as Donne was reacting against the self-conscious and self-indulgent adornment of popular Petrarchan poetry, Marvell can be read as mocking popular types of verse in his time – in particular, the *carpe diem* tradition. In his poem we have a comic portrayal in which foreplay would literally last for ages; this is followed by a frightening description of time as a 'winged chariot' and then by horrifying images, in which the effects of time are seen in a grave. Even the depiction of sex could be viewed as violent and disturbing: 'rough strife' between birds of prey that tear pleasure from each other and make time speed past.

As well as in the sixteenth and seventeenth centuries, the influence of the metaphysical poets can be felt in a wide range of later verse. In the post-1900 section of the *Anthology*, the most obvious example is Michael Symmons Roberts' 'To John Donne'. In this case, the poet uses or alludes to conceits from Donne's 'Elegy 19: To his Mistress Going to Bed'. What were once startling, clever and amusing uses of language now take on moribund tones as the intimate situation of two lovers has become debased in the light of a new form of colonisation.

Taking it further ▶

One of the best-known *carpe diem* poems is 'To the Virgins, to make much of time' by Robert Herrick. Conduct an internet search for this poem and compare it to 'To His Coy Mistress'. Pay particular attention to the ways in which the poets present time.

Note how the use of two updated metaphysical conceits structures the first part of the poem (the first nine stanzas). The first conceit extends to the fourth stanza as Roberts compares the woman's body to a territory that has been mapped. Yet the woman is not a sexual conquest for the man; both she and the man have already been conquered by the corporate powers that harness scientific research in the service of their profits. Unlike Donne's poem, where women's bodies are compared with a sense of delight to 'mystic books' (which are to be understood by appreciative and knowledgeable men), the map of the woman in Roberts' poem carries nothing more than functional information about illnesses: 'it is a textbook of disease'.

The second conceit compares the woman to America. Unlike the joyful, excited exclamation which led to further wondrous appreciation in Donne's poem, in 'To John Donne' the narrator's more muted address to the male lover – 'You call her your America' – is undercut by 'too right' and the comparison is extended to ugly images of colonisation and defending stolen property by force. While we can imagine Donne's original small audience of highly educated men being dazzled by his invention and wit, now Symmons Roberts' audience gains pleasure by recognising the allusions and in admiring the ways in which the contemporary poet updates Donne's language – even as they feel discomfort at the ideas with which he engages. The lack of metaphysical language in the last part of the poem – beginning 'Do you care?' – marks a more hopeful mood, and the tone towards the end of the poem seems much more warm and human than what went before. As well as this, religious and pastoral language help to cast off the weight of Donne, and the narrator gently and lovingly encourages the couple to rebel against the powers who conquered their bodies from within.

Sentiment

It is often revealing to consider the ways in which texts make you respond at an intellectual or at an emotional level; some, of course, can do both. Possibly the most heart-warming literary style – one which appeals primarily to the emotions – is known as **sentiment**. We are familiar with terms like 'sentimental' today, but their meanings have been subject to pejoration (that is, they have acquired negative connotations). For example, we might dismiss a film that overtly seeks to move us to tears or which shows characters openly discussing how much they care about each other (with emotional music playing in the background) as sentimental. Yet sentiment as understood in the eighteenth century was much more complex; as well as provoking fine feelings, it contains a moral dimension. It openly expresses tender feelings, places a high value on friendship and seeks to show sympathy; it is optimistic in its belief in the essential goodness of humankind. To experience sentimental feelings might involve luxuriating in your own feelings, but it could just as well mean to luxuriate and share with those of others. In this way, sentiment is morally beneficial since it not only encourages you to think generously of others, it encourages you to turn away from selfishness.

Burns' 'Ae Fond Kiss' was written in 1791, towards the end of what some critics call The Age of Sensibility, when sentimental literature was at its height. The form of the song is conducive towards an overt display of emotion and the subject matter – a pair of lovers parting – offers much scope for sentiment. Yet Burns' work is truly sentimental in that it is not just a wallowing in selfish emotion. After the first eight lines the speaker's focus moves from his own feelings to celebrate the woman he is soon to be parted from and to consider their joint feelings of love and affection. Thought of in the context of sentiment, it is possible to think of a true platonic love between the two, which – while perhaps having a thread or two of desire woven into the fabric of this pure type of love – need not have contained a sexual element. A biographical reading that considers Burns' promiscuity might put forward a different view, but looking at the speaker and his 'Nancie' in the words of the poem and through a prism of sentiment might persuade us that it is a purer kind of love. Fine sentimental feelings follow from the passionate declarations of love in the centre of the poem, with the speaker openly sharing sentimental emotions in language nearly identical to that used at the beginning, but before this cyclical conclusion, the poem climaxes on heartfelt and passionate good wishes to the woman who is leaving him:

> Fare-thee-weel, thou first and fairest!
> Fare-thee-weel, thou best and dearest!
> Thine be ilka joy and treasure,
> Peace, Enjoyment, Love and Pleasure!

While not sentimental in the same way as 'Ae Fond Kiss', some of the later poems in the pre-1900 section of the *Anthology* are worth considering from a sentimental perspective. Sentiment is often considered a precursor to Romanticism and 'She walks in beauty', a passionate lyric from Byron, a first generation Romantic poet, might be considered from a sentimental perspective. In a similar way, you might wish to consider the sentimental qualities – or at least the presentation of seemingly raw passion and emotion – in Ernest Dowson's 'Non Sum Qualis Eram Bonae sub Regno Cynarae', although it is worth bearing in mind that this poem with its Latin title and addressee sounds less obviously autobiographical than the other two. In addition, the feelings evoked by Dowson's poem might also be considered in their *fin de siècle* context – perhaps the poem articulates a yearning for the simplicity and goodness of sentimental feelings even as it languishes in the midst of a decadent lifestyle.

Satire

As well as sentiment, another literary style is often associated with the eighteenth century: satire. Satire might be thought of as a type of comedy, but one that aims at evoking more than laughter. Its method is often to mock a subject but with more than cruel intentions; satire mocks with a moral purpose. Satire comes in many varieties: Swift's *Gulliver's Travels*, for example, mocks many subjects, from comic mockery of particular politicians to quite a savage attack on human nature at large; Pope's *The Rape of the Lock* satirises the behaviour of overindulged aristocratic ladies with an amusing and deft touch. Satire can be seen in several of the poems in the anthologies. For instance, 'The Ruined Maid' is an amusing dramatisation of a country girl meeting a former friend who has become a fallen woman, but who has risen as a result. While obviously it could be argued that Hardy's primary purpose is to amuse and entertain, equally we could say that there is a serious subtext behind the laughter. Hardy does not intend those in his audience to become mistresses or prostitutes as a means to escape rural poverty; he wants us to laugh – not at the naive bumpkin who still labours in the village – but at the ridiculous double standard in Victorian sexual morality. While society kept up a stiff exterior and stigmatised sex before marriage, some estimates suggest that as many as 20 per cent of teenage women were forced into prostitution. Women who had sex before marriage were deemed fallen or ruined, but there was no such equivalent terminology for men. Indeed Hardy's mockery with a moral purpose might cause us to wonder who exactly in the poem is ruined: is it the 'fallen woman', or is it her former friend who has been ground down by the toil of rural labour which is a far cry from the pastoral images that we might like to associate with the countryside?

Poems that contain satirical elements are also found in the post-1900 section of the *Anthology*. For example, it could be said that Millay amuses the reader and, as she does so, mocks notions of male superiority. The opening lines – 'I being born a woman and distressed/By all the needs and notions of my kind' – articulate a conventionally sexist view of women. Note the alliterated 'n' sound that brings together 'needs' and 'notions', which along with 'distressed' presents a picture of women as delicate, emotionally fragile creatures, who are mentally weak, needy and subject to whims. Millay is obviously writing with a heavy dose of irony; the picture of women that emerges at the end of her sonnet is of anything but man-needing shrinking violets. The poem amuses us with its portrayal of the woman – not the man – who is subject to physical urges, but, after having satisfied them, wants to leave, thus satirising ideas that women grow dependent on men after sex, or are the ones who force them to settle down.

Millay makes satirical use of form, the sonnet – which is often associated with male speakers expressing their feelings and arguments associated with love – to present her ideas about the conflict between the mind and the body. Yet this female speaker emerges as being incredibly strong minded and decisive; we are in no doubt that it is her mind that triumphs at the end. Perhaps the poem could be read as a satirical riposte to earlier male poems of parting in which the male speaker either articulates his agony at having to leave his loved one, dressing up his deceptive intentions in gallantries and excuses about his need for new adventures. Unlike these poems, the speaker here is direct and unambiguous: sex was a spur of the moment mistake; our relationship is over; when we next meet, we don't even need to talk.

Literary periods and styles

Taking it further ▶

It is better to experience modernist texts for yourself than depend on the explanations of others. Why not read a little of two of the most celebrated works in prose and verse from the heyday of literary modernism in 1922: Joyce's *Ulysses* and Eliot's *The Waste Land*? Rather than begin at the beginning, you'll find it easier to start with Part II of *Ulysses* ('Mr Leopold Bloom ate with relish …').

Some literary contexts are associated with time periods, though their features may still be found in work from other times. For example, we might think of the following as being relevant to our study of the post-1900 poems: **modernism** (c. 1910–45) and **postmodernism** (c.1945–the present). These dates are not like those for a period such as World War I, which is always 1914–18; few critics agree on the exact times for each period. In addition, some texts from one period can have qualities of the other, so it is often sensible to consider each term as a particular style as much as a time period.

Modernism is the term given to texts from the early part of the twentieth century that self-consciously break away from earlier conventions, often taking the form of difficult, allusive and innovative writing. Consciousness is often a concern as modernist writers move away from the tradition of stable characters and objective narrators, sometimes depicting the ebb and flow of thought as they present narratives from the inside in self-conscious and subjective narrators. Time is often disrupted as characters experience not just present feelings, but also reflections, past emotions and thoughts of the future. In this way, readers experience a kind of writing that might be seen to offer a heightened form of experience – one that is more difficult for the reader to process, but which is perhaps a more accurate representation of how people actually experience life.

If we consider the poem written at the height of the modernist period, 'I, being born a woman' (1923), we see a poem that has little in common with the kinds of experiments that Eliot was popularising. Indeed, Millay considered herself a **lyric** poet and consciously rejected modernism; 'I, being born a woman', a Petrarchan sonnet, reflects her adherence to traditional forms. There is, however, a case that can be made for her ideas being in keeping with modernity. There is nothing traditional about the attitudes embodied in her sonnet, and some might suggest that Millay was able to combine respect for traditional aspects of poetic form with her more modern, progressive ideas.

Postmodernism

Like modernism, postmodernism is a broad era or cultural style that affects a wide range of artistic forms and beyond. The titles of some of the most influential works on the subject attest to its pervasive nature: for example, Jean-Francois Lyotard's *The Postmodern Condition* explores how postmodernism can be seen in areas as wide as science, the arts and technology, and Fredric Jameson's study *Postmodernism* is subtitled 'Or the Cultural Logic of Late Capitalism' and considers it as a historical period. The features that Jameson identifies as being typical of a postmodern style are useful to consider when viewing texts as postmodern. They include aspects such as the following:

- depthlessness
- pastiche (the imitation of a previous form, or the mixing of several forms)

- the fragmentation of the subject
- the collapsing of the boundary between high and low culture.

To think about postmodernism as a style it might be helpful to think about popular film. For example, *Pulp Fiction* (1994), directed by Quentin Tarantino, makes use of a range of different artistic forms, from classic Hollywood and French New Wave films to surfer music and thinly-drawn characters from cheap crime novels (hence the pulp fiction of the title). Stylistically, the film is complex and bears critical analysis – for example, the plot memorably starts near the end of the story and ends just after the place where it began. Yet, beneath the surface sheen, the film might be said to lack depth; unlike modernist art forms, it seems to relate more to other art (predominantly film and popular culture) than it does to life and it does so in a playful rather than serious fashion.

Postmodern features can be seen in several of the poems from the post-1900 part of the *Anthology*. For example, Tony Harrison makes the Meredithian sonnet his own in a touching tribute to the love of his parents in 'Timer'. While much of the metre and rhyme have been retained, the sonnet is broken up into scattered stanzas that enable the poet to place emphasis on certain moments in the story and on particular images. The poem embraces the complexities of high culture not only in its form, but in its symbolism, which includes the burnished ring and the hour glass; yet its language is predominantly accessible (with, for example, the simple reported speech of the father and the idiomatic direct speech of the crematorium clerk).

Muldoon's 'Long Finish' and Duffy's 'The Love Poem' are arguably even more postmodern in their style. While Muldoon's ballade is obviously a love poem and one written in a self-consciously poetic tradition, it also embraces a wide range of reference with allusions to everything from economics to a fourteenth-century Japanese play and from wine tasting to medicine for eczema. The way in which the narrative blends one subject in to another and from past to present is a further postmodern feature. At one moment Muldoon's poem is focused on his wife and her body, the next it has slipped into thoughts and images of violence in Northern Ireland – while scarcely losing its fluent pace and wry tone. In this way, a playful, romantic moment blends almost seamlessly into a narrative of assassination, with the two separate experiences blended by a single sentence that stretches across two enjambed fourth and fifth stanzas.

The light touch of the postmodern poet makes it difficult for the reader to know how to respond. Unlike the weighty reflections of Heaney's speaker in 'Punishment' who encourages the reader to consider the moral complexities of the atrocity in question, Muldoon's representation of violence is unexpected and without authorial comment. It is unclear where the images have come from: whether they are imagined images summoned by television of news reports or from personal experience. In the fifth stanza, there is something shocking about the use of the refrain – 'and then some'— which in the first referred playfully to overfilling a glass with good wine; now it refers to a gratuitous act of killing. Whether we think about the omnipresence of violence, how thoughts of it rise up unbidden at the least likely time, or how it leaves a visual aftershock, or affects a Northern Irish person even when they are on the other side of the world, the violence registers with the reader in both puzzling and disturbing ways.

Carol Ann Duffy's 'The Love Poem' is another obviously postmodern poem. It has an extremely **intertextual** nature, to the extent where it relates to other poems more than it relates to specific external events. Even the parts that are not taken from other poems are self-referential, such as 'love's lips pursed to a question mark' or love's light fading, darkening,/black as ink on a page'. By so doing, though, it celebrates writing and love poetry through the ages as well as – like Shakespeare's 'Sonnet 116' – the enduring joys of love itself.

Working with the text

Assessment Objectives and skills

> **AO1** Articulate informed, personal and creative responses to literary texts, using associated concepts and terminology, and coherent, accurate written expression.

To do well with AO1 you need to write fluently, structuring your essay carefully, guiding your reader clearly through your line of argument and using the sophisticated vocabulary, including appropriate critical terminology. Use frequent embedded quotations to show detailed knowledge and demonstrate familiarity with the whole text. Your aim is to produce a well written academic essay employing appropriate discourse markers to create the sense of a shaped argument; it should use sophisticated terminology at times while remaining clear and cohesive.

> **AO2** Analyse ways in which meanings are shaped in literary texts.

Strong students do not work only on a lexical level, but write well on the generic and structural elements, so it is often useful to start by analysing those larger elements of narrative organisation before considering the poets' use of language. If 'form is meaning', what are the implications of this for each poem? Then again, to discuss language in detail you need to quote from poems, analyse what you quote and use such analysis to illuminate your argument. Moreover, since, at times, you need to make points about generic and organisational features, being able to reference closely and effectively is just as important as mastering the art of the embedded quotation. Practise writing in analytical sentences, comprising a brief quotation or close reference, a definition or description of the feature you intend to analyse, an explanation of how this feature has been used and an evaluation of its effectiveness.

> **AO3** Demonstrate understanding of the significance and influence of the contexts in which literary texts are written and received.

To access AO3 you need to think about how contexts of production, reception, literature, culture, biography, geography, society, history, genre and **intertextuality** can affect texts. Place each poem at the heart of a web of contextual factors which you feel have had the most impact upon it; examiners want to see a sense of contextual alertness woven seamlessly into the fabric of your essay rather than a clumsy bolted-on website rehash or some recycled history notes. Show you understand that literary works contain encoded representations of the cultural, moral, religious, racial and political values of the society from which they emerged, and that over time attitudes and ideas change until the views they reflect are no longer widely shared.

> **A04** Explore connections across literary texts.

If your examination requires you to compare and contrast one or more other texts with *the Anthology* you must try to find specific points of comparison, rather than merely generalising. You will find it easier to make connections between texts if you try to balance them as you write; remember also that connections are not only about finding similarities – differences are just as interesting. Above all, consider how the comparison illuminates each text; some connections will be thematic, others generic or stylistic.

> **A05** Explore literary texts informed by different interpretations.

For this AO, you should refer to the opinions of critics and remain alert to aspects of the poems which are open to interpretation. Your job is to measure your own interpretation of the text against those of other readers. Try to convey an awareness of multiple readings as well as an understanding that (as Barthes suggested) a text's meaning is dependent as much upon what you bring to it as what the poet left there. Using modal verb phrases such as 'may be seen as', 'might be interpreted as' or 'could be represented as' shows you know that different readers interpret texts in different ways at different times. The key word here is plurality; there is no single meaning or one right answer. Relish getting your teeth into the views of published critics to push forward your own argument, but always keep in mind that meanings in poems are shifting and unstable as opposed to fixed and permanent.

Summary

Overall, the hallmarks of a successful A-level essay that hits all five AOs include:

- a clear introduction which orientates the reader and outlines your main argument
- a coherent and conceptualised argument which relates to the question title
- confident movement around the text or texts rather than a relentless chronological trawl
- apt and effective quotations or references adapted to make sense within the context of your own sentence
- a range of effective points about the poets' dramatic methods
- a strong and personally engaged understanding of how a text can be interpreted by different readers and audiences in different ways at different times
- a sense that you are prepared to take on a good range of critical and theoretical perspectives
- a conclusion that consolidates your response and relates it back to your essay title.

Building skills 1: Structuring your writing

This Building skills section focuses upon organising your written responses to convey your ideas as clearly and effectively as possible: the 'how' of your writing as opposed to the 'what'. More often than not, if your knowledge and understanding of your chosen section of the *Anthology* is sound, a disappointing mark or grade will be down to one of two common mistakes: misreading the question or failing to organise your response economically and effectively. In an examination you'll be lucky if you can demonstrate 5 per cent of what you know; luckily, if it's the right 5 per cent, that's all you need to gain full marks.

Understanding your examination

It's important to prepare for the specific type of response with regard to your chosen section from the *AQA Anthology: love poetry through the ages*. If you are studying the text for AS, you will be invited to evaluate a viewpoint and comment closely on a single poem. For A-level, you compare poems from your chosen section of the *Anthology* to the novel that you have chosen as part of the Love through the Ages theme.

For AS, each question will focus on a single poem, which will be reprinted in the question paper. For A-level, you can take a clean, unannotated copy of the *Anthology* and a copy of your chosen novel into the examination room. Since you have the text (or texts) in front of you, you have every opportunity to quote relevantly, accurately and extensively. To gain a high mark, you are expected to focus in detail on specific parts of the text. Remember, too, that you must not refer to any supporting material such as a scholarly introduction. If an examiner suspects that you have been copying chunks of unacknowledged material from such a source, they will refer your paper to the examining body for possible plagiarism.

Responding to examination questions

Step 1: Planning and beginning: locate the debate

A very common type of exam question invites you to open up a debate about the text by using various trigger words and phrases such as **'examine the view that …'** or **'how far do you agree with this view?'** When analysing this type of question, the one thing you can be sure of is that exam questions never offer a view that makes no sense at all or one so blindingly obvious all anyone can do is agree with it; there will always be a genuine interpretation at stake. So logically your introduction needs to address the terms of this debate and sketch out the outlines of how you intend to move the argument forward to orientate the reader. Since it's obviously going to be helpful if you actually know this before you start writing, you really do need to plan before you begin to write.

Undertaking a lively debate about some of the ways in which the poems of your chosen section of the *Anthology* have been and can be interpreted is the DNA of your essay. Of course any good argument needs to be honest; to begin by writing 'yes, I totally agree with this obviously true statement' suggests a fundamental misunderstanding of what studying literature is all about. The given views in examination questions are designed to open up critical conversations, not shut them down.

Plan your answer by collecting together points for and against the given view. Aim to see a stated opinion as an interesting way of focusing upon a key facet of the *Anthology* or the poem under discussion, like the following student.

Student A

This student is answering an AS examination task in the style of AQA Specification A, which works with a given view. The question, which is clearly designed to open up a debate, is:

'Examine the view that in 'Meeting Point' MacNeice is interested in art – showing a beautiful frozen moment in time – rather than real love featuring a real couple.'

The question, to my mind, expresses fundamental truths about the poem, but as I will argue in this essay, it is not a question of either/or, but of both/and. Of course, MacNeice is interested in art – his poem includes, for example, many arresting and unusual images – but it is also concerned to show real people in a real historical context. For example, he uses details such as the couple 'Not caring if the markets crash' to show them as real people from a real time – in this case in the 1930s and in the Depression that came in the wake of the Wall Street Crash. This suggests that not even the biggest problems of society – those which affected practically the whole world – can affect them, thus highlighting the strength of their love.

To turn more closely to the details of the poem, we can see how MacNeice both creates aesthetic pleasure for the reader through his construction of beautiful frozen moments and he presents the realities of the real couple's experience. In the poem's very first stanza, MacNeice includes realistic details of the coffee shop, such as the 'two glasses' and the 'two chairs', and these details are used to introduce the real love that the couple feels. As well as continuing the semantic field of numbers to pleasingly introduce the idea of the love between 'two people with the one pulse', MacNeice plays with ideas that stretch back to Plato's symposium – humans originally had four arms and legs, but fearing their power Zeus ripped them apart, condemning them to forever seek their other half. If love is the name for the pursuit of wholeness, it seems to have found its consummation in this moment of wholeness as artfully described by MacNeice. The line that describes the unity is given prominence not only by it being the central line in this five-line stanza, but also by it being enveloped by two pairs of rhyming lines. The pleasing aural and structural effects are also amplified by its echo with the refrain, since 'And two people with the one pulse' half rhymes with 'Time was away and somewhere else'.

Thus, it could be argued that MacNeice is both interested in art and reality. Though the kind of reality he shows, it must be conceded, is subtly changed to match the experience of time frozen love that he evokes. It is not so much that MacNeice shows the ordinary but that he shows how the ordinary can become transformed into the extraordinary by love ...

Examiner's commentary

This student:

- ❚ deftly takes on the central premise of the question from the outset
- ❚ expresses a confident and original personal view
- ❚ keeps returning to the question's key terms: 'art' (which becomes 'artfully'), 'frozen moment', 'real' (which sometimes becomes 'realistic' or 'ordinary') and 'suppression'
- ❚ deals with some key features of AO2 in terms of poetic methods
- ❚ creates a convincing, fluent and well-supported argument
- ❚ quotes frequently and appositely, ranging across the text well to select the most useful short phrases to support the argument
- ❚ applies the contextual idea from Plato in a relevant and developed manner.

If the rest of the essay reached this level of performance, it is likely she would be on course to achieve a notional grade A.

Step 2: Developing and linking: go with the flow

An essay is a very specific type of formal writing that requires an appropriate discourse structure. In the main body of your writing, you need to thread your developing argument through each paragraph consistently and logically, referring back to the terms established by the question itself, rephrasing and reframing as you go. It can be challenging to sustain the flow of your essay and keep firmly on track, but here are some techniques to help you.

- Ensure your essay doesn't disintegrate into a series of disconnected building blocks by creating a neat and stable bridge between one paragraph and the next.

- Use discourse markers – linking words and phrases like 'on the other hand', 'however', 'although' and 'moreover' – to hold the individual paragraphs of your essay together and signpost the connections between different sections of your overarching argument.

- Having set out an idea in Paragraph A, in Paragraph B you might need to then support it by providing a further example; if so, signal this to your reader with a phrase such as '**Moreover**, this idea is developed in the next two stanzas …'

- To change direction and challenge an idea begun in Paragraph A by acknowledging that it is open to interpretation, you could begin Paragraph B with something like '**On the other hand**, this view of the text could be challenged by a feminist critic …'

- Another typical paragraph-to-paragraph link is when you want to show that the original idea doesn't give the full picture. Here you could modify your original point with something like '**Although** it is possible to see the realistic elements within the poem, it could be argued that by MacNeice's poetic methods, he distorts the real into the ideal, but it could equally be argued that this is a reflection of the power of real love.'

Step 3: Concluding: seal the deal

As you bring your writing to a close, you need to capture and clarify your response to the given view and make a relatively swift and elegant exit. Keep your final paragraph short and sweet. Now is not the time to introduce any new points – but equally, don't just reword everything you have already just said either. Neat potential closers include:

- looping the last paragraph back to something you mentioned in your introduction to suggest that you have now said all there is to say on the subject

- reflecting on your key points in order to reach a balanced overview

- ending with a punchy quotation that leaves the reader thinking

- discussing the contextual implications of the topic you have debated

- reversing expectations to end on an interesting alternative view

- stating why you think the main issue or theme under discussion is so central to the poems

- mentioning how different audiences over time might have responded to the topic you have been debating.

Student B

This student is concluding the same AS examination task that Student A was working on:

'Examine the view that in 'Meeting Point' MacNeice is interested in art – showing a beautiful frozen moment in time – rather than real love featuring a real couple.'

The meeting point, therefore, we might say both spiritual and physical, and in both respects the two so-in-love lovers are linked through their urge to escape from modern life, the Wall Street Crash and all that jazz. I agree that the moment is amazing and beautiful and – as I noted above – some of the images, such as the bell which transforms into a flower, stand out, with both an unusual and a familiar element, not to say metaphysical conceit sort of way. This is very relevant to the main idea of the poem. This is an ordinary situation, but the emotional buzz between the people, who have met together at this point is amazing or magical even. To take issues with the second part of the question, I would like to say 'how can any poem show real love since the act of artistic production necessarily involves artifice?' It may not be real in the sense that it's not meant to be – how can water flow from a rock? I don't think MacNeice wanted us to read this as a real situation involving real people. It might even have been him and a girlfriend having a quick coffee after a day at the office. So, despite disagreeing with the view I also agree, but in a different way.

Examiner's commentary

This student:

▼ attempts to introduce relevant contextual material (to do with the Wall Street Crash and with the later assertive biographical reference). Such references are introduced rather clumsily and are not made wholly relevant

▼ uses a strong example from the text – about the bell and the flower – but weakens the point by bringing in the detail about the metaphysical conceit (which perhaps could have been used well in the main body of the essay)

▼ grapples with the key words of the question: the student writes directly about beauty and realism

- ◣ has a flexible vocabulary, which includes some advanced phrasing such as 'artistic production necessarily involves artifice'
- ◣ has a rather prolix (wordy) style of expression. Some of the sentences lack control and there are informal turns of phrase such as the 'so-in-love lovers', 'the emotional buzz' and the attempt at humour ('and all that jazz') doesn't quite work in this context.

Despite the flaws in expression, some of the ideas are strong. The student questions how a poem can be termed realistic as well as comments on images that are both ordinary and extraordinary and links such details to the poem's overall meaning.

If the rest of the examination answer reached this level of performance, it would be on course to achieve a notional grade C. Although, with greater focus, concision and clarity of language the answer would have the potential to move higher on the mark scheme.

Building skills 2: Analysing texts in detail

Having worked through Building skills 1 on structuring your writing, this section of the guide contains a range of annotated extracts from students' responses. The next few pages enable you to assess the extent to which these students have successfully demonstrated their writing skills and mastery of the Assessment Objectives to provide you with an index by which to measure your own skills progress. Each extract comes with a commentary to help you identify what each student is doing well and/or what changes they would need to make to their writing to target a higher grade.

The main focus here is on the ways in which you can successfully include within your own well-structured writing clear and appropriate references to both your chosen section of the *Anthology* and the ways in which other readers have responded. In an examination, of course, the 'other reading' you need to refer to consistently is encoded within the question itself: the 'given view' in other words.

Student A

This student is in the middle of answering an A-level examination task in the style of AQA Specification A, which invites comparisons between the *Anthology* and a set novel (*Wuthering Heights*):

Compare how the authors of two texts you have studied present the loss of love.

It might be argued that some of the differences in the ways that loss is presented in Wuthering Heights and in the poetry from the AQA Anthology of Love Poems through the Ages (post-1900) spring from those between the genres of prose and verse. The space of the novel allows for greater character development and perhaps more dramatic incidents. For example, in his reactions to the death of Cathy, we see several sides to Heathcliff's character. Nelly's narrative is at pains to portray him as a man struggling with grief. She describes how 'he trembled, in spite of himself, to his very finger-ends and begins to empathise with him, encouraging Lockwood (and, by extension, the reader) to share her feelings: '"Poor wretch!" I thought; "you have a heart and nerves the same as your brother men! Why should you be so anxious to conceal them? Your pride cannot blind God! You tempt him to wring them, till he forces a cry of humiliation!"' There is much irony in those lines as the reader comes to realise that she is projecting on to Heathcliff fine feelings and Christian values that he does not share. She continues in the same vein, describing the death of Catherine in idealized terms: '"She lies with a sweet smile on her face; and her latest ideas wandered back to her pleasant early days. Her life closed in a gentle dream – may she wake as kindly in the other world!"' When Heathcliff replies, Brontë effects a sharp shift in tone: '"May she wake in torment!" He cried, with frightful vehemence, stamping his foot, and groaning in a sudden paroxysm of ungovernable passion. "Why she's a liar to the end! Where is she? Not *there* – not in heaven – not perished – where?"' and his speech goes on to utter a dark prayer for Cathy never to rest as long as he lives and for her to haunt him. It culminates in the famous lines: '"I cannot live without my life! I cannot life without my soul!"' The sheer violence of the emotions is compelling (and perhaps shocking for a mid-nineteenth-century reader) as civilized notions such as not speaking ill of the dead are exploded and Brontë's Byronic hero takes on a darker satanic dimension, rejecting ideas of Christian comfort and blasphemously praying to be haunted. Yet, paradoxically, the violence of his emotions and the venom of his words allow the reader to appreciate the force and depth of his love, which Brontë reinforces through Nelly's descriptions as 'He dashed his head against the knotted trunk; and, lifting up his eyes, howled, not like a man, but like a savage beast getting goaded to death with knives and spears.'

While such melodramatic and extreme language presents love with much spelled out for the reader, the concision and suggestive power of poetry often allows more room for more of the reader's own feelings. For example, poems such as 'Vergissmeinnicht' and 'A Quoi Bon Dire' offer more gentle presentations of the effects of loss. While the language describing the body of the dead German gunner is grotesque and replete with vivid images of the decomposing corpse (which are much harder-hitting than Nelly's descriptions of Cathy's death and how she fell into 'a gentle dream'), it is the reactions of the living that contrast most. Heathcliff's dialogue is full of cries, exclamations, emphasis and stuttering strong emotion; the confrontation between Steffi and death is imagined, not dramatised directly, and it is gentle and poetic. While there is subtle alliteration and assonance as well as the gentle regular beat of the iambic tetrameter; the respectful sound of the words is at odds with the horror the images depict:

But she would weep to see today
How on his skin the swart flies move
The dust upon the paper eye
And the burst stomach like a cave.

Unlike the reader's acquaintance with Heathcliff and Catherine – we know the circumstances of the childhood, about their separation and so on – there is much for the reader to do to imagine the lives of Steffi and the German soldier, and yet readers are still able to appreciate their loss. There is a strong sense of universality in this loss – something that is not felt in our reading of the loss of Cathy. Douglas uses his last stanza to amplify this broader significance, personifying death and elevating the different roles of the German gunner to the level of archetypes:

For here the lover and the killer are mingled
who had one body and one heart.
And death who had the soldier singled
Has done the lover mortal hurt.

Perhaps the autobiographical nature of the poem – which was based on a real incident that took place when Douglas was commanding a tank in North Africa – helps to make the sense of loss poignant, real and applicable to many in wartime situations, whereas the loss experienced by Heathcliff is dramatic, entertaining and thought-provoking in the confines of its context as a nineteenth-century novel. The mix of the Gothic and the Romantic in Brontë is largely escapist as we imagine the lives of characters defined by extremes, while the horror and the romance in 'Vergissmeinnicht' is not just based on real life, but is all too real.

Examiner's commentary

This student:

❧ realises that the focus of the essay is on loss and chooses poems and an incident from the novel that deal with loss – in this case through death and bereavement

❧ uses the authors' names as the makers of textual meaning frequently when analysing characterisation and methods

❧ forges a very clear link between the two paragraphs, developing the same idea and comparing how it is presented in the second text

❧ comments on the reader as a maker of meaning, considering how readers at different times might have responded

❧ embeds short, relevant quotations seamlessly, so that the flow of his writing is not disrupted

❧ quotes frequently and always relevantly – just a few well-chosen words being enough at times, but also using longer quotations which are followed by more detailed analysis

❧ uses a flexible, critical vocabulary, with critical terms that help the writer to achieve precision and concision as well as achieve a consistently analytical style.

If the rest of the examination answer reached this level of performance, it is likely the student would be on course to achieve a notional grade A.

Student B

This student is answering an A-level examination task in the style of AQA Specification A, which invites comparisons between the *Anthology* and a set novel (*Tess of the D'Urbervilles*):

Compare how the authors of two texts you have studied present infidelity.

There are many types of infidelity in the Anthology, ranging from the speaker who has strayed from his true love but makes the excuse that he has been 'faithful to thee, Cynara, in my fashion' to the speaker in 'Absent from Thee' who is being honest about what he wants to do with other women, but still feels strong affection for the woman he addresses. Tess of the D'Urbervilles offers attitudes to infidelity that seem unusual to today's readers. Why can't she just love him, we might say, but to people of Hardy's time Tess having already formed a sexual union with Alec makes her seem like an adultress when she marries Angel.

I think many men want to have it both ways: they want to party and be with many women, but they also want to have the comfort and security of a steady girlfriend. In that way Ernest Dowson's 'Non sum qualis eram bonae sub regno Cynarae' expresses both a fin de siècle sensibility and a modern one. The sensory overload of the descriptions of the partying lifestyle of the speaker give the reader a sense of decadence and of being fed up with such a life: there are 'kisses and the wine', 'roses riotously' flung and 'madder music and stronger wine', for example. Each of these things in itself might be pleasing, but we have a sense that together they are overwhelming. The party lifestyle is not helping him; he is not enjoying it and it comes across as too much. There is an irony underneath it that the speaker is actually pining for his true love, Cynara. The fact that he uses the refrain shows this but it also means he is admitting that he is guilty. The guilt over his unfaithfulness, I think, is reflected in his lifestyle which is actually a vicious circle: he feels guilty at his infidelity, so he goes out to forget but ends up doing it again.

Tess also feels guilty for her behaviour, and like Dowson's speaker, she is untruthful with herself. All throughout the courtship with Angel, she feels guilt over her secret affair with Alec but tries to repress it and the reader has a feeling she will for several chapters until circumstances mean that she does not tell Angel and she must be married with the burden of the guilt weighing down on her. Hardy uses many techniques to foreshadow the eventual doom when Angel finds out and loses it over what he sees as Tess's unfaithfulness as he believes that Tess through having had sex with Alex is married to him in the eyes of God. Angel though embodies the Victorian double standard by telling Tess about his pre-marital sexual exploits but when she tells him what she did it doesn't matter — in matters of sexual morality even in late Victorian England it is as Hardy's phase title for the section of the novel after her revelation, 'The Woman Pays.'

Examiner's commentary

This student:

- has relevant ideas concerning attitudes to infidelity in different times, though these are sometimes expressed using colloquial language, such as 'cheated on' and 'the party lifestyle'

- makes helpful analytical comments, such as 'the sensory overload' giving the 'reader a sense of decadence', but some of the evidence is listed and might have been explored in greater depth

- the comments on the literary periods of the texts – for example, the 'fin de siècle' context of Dowson and the late Victorian attitudes to sexual morality – cast light on the texts; more use of such ideas, with further textual detail would help to lift this answer higher on the mark scheme

- there is linking of ideas, but while the second paragraph (about Tess) does have links to what was argued about the Dowson poem above, the comparisons and contrasts are not fully developed and there is no explicit exploration of links at the level of authorial methods.

If the rest of the examination answer reached this level of performance, it is likely the student would be on course to achieve a notional grade C.

Glossary

addressee – the person the speaker addresses in the poem

alexandrine – a line of iambic hexameter (twelve syllables, comprised of six iambic feet). Thought to originate in twelfth-century French Romances about Alexander the Great, alexandrines became common in later French dramatic and narrative poetry

allegory – a narrative with two distinct levels of meaning. For example, Orwell's *Animal Farm* is, on one level, a story about animals who rebel against their farmer and set up their own system of running the farm; on a deeper level, it is about the Russian people rising up against their ruler and developing communism as the means of government

allusion – an indirect reference made that relies on the reader's prior knowledge. For example, when Michael Symmons Roberts writes of ' – your roving hands – ' in 'To John Donne' he alludes to John Donne's 'To His Mistress Going to Bed', specifically, the clause 'license my roving hands'

apostrophe – an address to a person, **personification** or abstraction who is not present

archaic – outdated language; words and phrases are considered archaic if they have passed out of common usage before the time of writing

assonance – the repetition of vowel sounds in nearby words

ballade – a poem comprised of three **octaves** (eight-line **stanzas**) rhymed ababbcbc, followed by a further four lines, known as an envoi, which is rhymed bcbc. It also has a **refrain** (a repeated line), which is the first line of the first stanza and the final line of subsequent stanzas

blazon – the poetic tradition of cataloguing the woman's features, often moving down her body

caesura – a definite break in the middle of a line of verse; it is usually, but not always, indicated by a punctuation mark

carpe diem – this term comes from the Latin for 'seize the day' and a *carpe diem* poem is one in which the speaker urges the addressee to seize the day – that is, to make the most of the present.

conceit – a striking extended metaphor that compares two elements that at first seem very dissimilar

confessional poetry – poetry in which the poet uses private or intimate details of his or her life as subject matter

couplet – two lines that are rhymed and are usually of equal length and rhythm

cross-rhyme – the use of alternately rhyming lines; for example, in a **quatrain** that rhymes abab

end-stopped – a line is end stopped when it concludes with a punctuation mark

English (or Shakespearean) sonnet – see **sonnet**

enjambed – a line is enjambed when it does not conclude with a punctuation mark

envelope rhyme – a type of rhyme in which a line or group of lines is enclosed by lines that rhyme, for example, in each of the stanzas in a five-line stanza rhymed abcba. This can have the effect of making the line or lines that are enveloped stand out

eponymous – the eponymous character is the one with the same name as the title

exclamatory – a sentence that expresses an exclamation (such as a cry, a shout or some other strong and sudden emotion

feminine ending – when a line ends on an unstressed syllable (when a line ends on a stressed syllable it is a masculine ending)

feminine rhyme – a rhyme, that falls on an unstressed syllable (a masculine rhyme falls on a stressed syllable)

free verse – a type of verse that has no set metrical or rhyming pattern

Gothic – a genre associated with an author's desire to horrify, terrify or thrill. It typically features monstrous or disturbed characters and uses settings such as ruined castles, graveyards and dungeons

hexameter – a line of verse with six metrical units (a line of **iambic hexameter** – also called an alexandrine – has twelve syllables)

iamb – a metrical unit comprised of an unstressed syllable followed by a stressed one

imagery – words that summon sensory perceptions in the reader's mind. This could be in the form of visual images, but it could also involve one of the other senses – for example, the perception of a smell or a sound or a feeling

internal rhyme – a rhyme in which at least one of the rhyming words is positioned somewhere other than the end of the line

intertextual – the quality of a text relating to other texts. When you explore the meanings and effects that are produced by a text's relationships to other texts, you are exploring intertextuality

lyric – a relatively short, non-narrative poem that expresses the mood or thoughts and feelings of the speaker

Meredithian sonnet – a sonnet of 16 lines usually comprised of four **quatrains**. The extra two lines allow for the development of the idea or the narrative, thus avoiding the predictability or overly neat feeling that the conclusion of an English or Petrarchan sonnet can bring

metaphysical – a style of poetry popularised by poets like Donne in the late 1500s. It is marked by its wit, intellectualism and by the way in which it uses **conceits**: elaborate metaphors that draw similarities between elements that at first seem wildly dissimilar

metre – the rhythm of a poem. There are many different types of metre according to the sequence of unstressed and stressed syllables (which you might think of as light and heavy beats) used and the number of units of metre in the line. The most common metres are easy to recognise. For example, you probably know **iambic pentameter** – the most common metre in Shakespearean verse. It has five (*pent* – means five in Greek) iambic units (a stressed syllable followed by an unstressed syllable). **Iambic tetrameter** is an eight-syllable line comprised of four iambs (*tetra* – meaning four in Greek); **iambic dimeter** is a four-syllable line, divided into two iambic units

Modernism – a self-consciously new (or modern) and artistic style associated with the early twentieth century. Modernist texts break away from earlier conventions, often taking the form of difficult, allusive and innovative writing (see p.76 for further discussion)

monosyllabic – having one syllable

octave – a stanza of eight lines

paradox – a statement that seems to contradict itself, but which usually expresses a truth

parallelism – the arrangement of groups of words or lines with similar word order. It can suggest a correspondence of meaning, or draw attention to a contrast

pastoral – from `pastor', the Latin for shepherd, a literary genre that features idealised representations of the countryside

patriarchal – from patriarchy (literally `ruling father'), which refers to a system whereby men have control over women; such power may be exerted directly or in more subtle ways

pentameter – see **metre**

personification – the device by which inanimate things or abstract concepts are written about as though they are human. For example, in morality plays a character might be the personification of a sin such as Lust or Greed. Personification involves a more fully formed representation of a person than pathetic fallacy, which is when an aspect of the natural world takes on a human emotion, for example, the storm raged

Petrarchan sonnet – see **sonnet**

popular culture – forms of entertainment and leisure activities that are widely consumed by many, such as film, television, pop music and so on, rather than art forms that are enjoyed by an educated few

postmodernism – usually associated with the period since 1945, postmodern texts often have strong elements of pastiche and intertextuality; they usually mix elements of high and low culture, have a sense of depthlessness and often feature a fragmented narrative and/or an unreliable narrator (see p.76 for further discussion)

quatrain – a stanza of four lines

refrain – a repeated line, part of a line or group of lines. It may have slight variations

satire – a type of humour in which the writer mocks someone or something, but with a moral purpose. This might, for example, involve revealing the follies of human nature, or ridiculing someone in power to undermine their position

semantic field – a group of words that have similar meanings, or, more loosely, are drawn from the same topic area. For example, close study of a poem might reveal a semantic field of war or conflict

sestet – a stanza of six lines

sonnet – a lyric poem, usually of 14 lines. There are two main types of sonnet: the **Petrarchan**, which contains a stanza of eight lines (an **octave**) after which there is a change of mood or sudden shift in the argument of the poem (a **volta**) then a further six lines (the **sestet**), and the **English (or Shakepearean)**, which has three lines of four (three **quatrains**) and a final two lines that rhyme (a **couplet**)

speaker – the one who speaks the poem. It is wise to use this as the default term when discussing a poem. Keep 'narrator' for one telling a story and 'persona' for a speaker who is clearly not the poet

stanza – a group of lines within a poem, usually – but not always – separated by white space

stanzaic form – the shape and structure of the stanzas

subgenre – a specific subsection within a larger genre. For example, confessional poetry is often considered to be a subgenre of autobiography

symbol – one thing that stands for another, broader idea. For example, the cross is a symbol of Christianity. While a metaphorical language usually traces a correspondence between things and is often clear in its intention, symbolism works by suggestion and is often much more ambiguous – its meanings are more open

tercet – a stanza of three lines

tetrameter – see **metre**

triplet – a stanza of three lines all of which rhyme

trochee – a metrical unit in which a stressed syllable is followed by an unstressed syllable

trope – from the Greek for a turn, any literary device in which words are used in ways other than their literal meaning. For example, a metaphor is a type of trope. The term is also used for a commonly recurring device or situation with which readers and audiences are likely to be familiar

verse paragraph – a block of verse forming a clearly defined part of a poem. As in prose, its length is determined by the topic being explored, or the part of the story being told

volta – from the Latin for 'turn', a volta is the point at which there is a marked shift in tone, change of subject or development of the argument in a sonnet. (Reserve this term for discussions of sonnets; avoid using it for shifts in other types of poem.)

zeugma – when a single verb qualifies two nouns with different senses, such as in 'Anna! … "Dost sometimes counsel take—and sometimes tea."' The verb 'take' qualifies 'counsel' (she sometimes takes advice) and 'tea' (she sometimes takes tea)

Taking it further

Books

- Baldick, C. (2008) *The Oxford Dictionary of Literary Terms*, Oxford University Press
  - An easy-to-use glossary, with entries on styles and movements as well as literary terms.
- Lennard, L. (2005) *The Poetry Handbook*, Oxford University Press
  - Suitable for more advanced criticism, this book contains detailed discussions of all aspects of poetry.
- Matterson and Jones (2010) *Studying Poetry*, Bloomsbury
  - An excellent guide to appreciating poetry that includes contextual and theoretical approaches in an accessible, integrated way.
- Booth, S (ed.) (1980) *Shakespeare's Sonnets*, Yale University Press
- Burnett, A. (ed.) (2012) *The Complete Poems of Philip Larkin*, Faber & Faber
- Fisher, N. (ed.) (2000) *That Second Bottle, Essays on the Earl of Rochester*, Manchester University Press
- Graham, D. (ed.) (1990) *Keith Douglas the Complete Poems*, Oxford University Press
- Heaney, S. (1984) 'Feeling into Words' in *Preoccupations*, Faber and Faber
- Larkin, P. (1982) 'Philip Larkin, The Art of Poetry No. 30,' *The Paris Review*
- Longley, E. (1988) *Louis MacNeice A Study*, Faber & Faber
- Longley, E. (1996) *Poetry in the Wars*, Bloodaxe
- Luft, J. 'Roberts's "To John Donne" and Donne's "Elegy 19"', *The Explicator*, Vol. 68, No. 2
- McClatchy, J.D. (1978) *Anne Sexton: The Artist and her Critics*, Indiana University Press
- Patterson, D. (2012) *101 Sonnets*, Faber & Faber
  - This anthology contains an interesting introduction, written in a lively, engaging and informative style.
- Pope, A. (1717) *A Discourse on Pastoral Poetry* in Croker (ed.) (1871), *The Works of Alexander Pope Vol. I*, John Murray
- Preminger, A. and Brogan, T.V.F. (1993) *The New Princeton Encyclopedia of Poetry and Poetics*, Princeton University Press
  - The most detailed and definitive guide to poetic terms.
- Salusinszky, I. (ed.) (2005) *Northrop Frye's Writings on the Eighteenth and Nineteenth Centuries*, University of Toronto Press

◥ Schmidt, M. (1998) *Lives of the Poets*, Orion
◥ Waterman, R. (2014) *Belonging and Estrangement in the Poetry of Philip Larkin, R S Thomas and Charles Causley*, Ashgate

Weblinks

◥ Carol Ann Duffy, quoted in The Poetry Archive at:
www.poetryarchive.org/poet/carol-ann-duffy
  – The site also includes numerous recordings and a wealth of information about poets and poetry.

◥ Carolyn Burdett, 'Aestheticism and Decadence' at:
www.bl.uk/romantics-and-victorians/articles/aestheticism-and-decadence

◥ Clive James, *Reading for Life*, 2006 at:
www.clivejames.com/poetry-notebook/5

◥ www.bbc.co.uk/arts/robertburns

  – An excellent, comprehensive site about Burns and his work, featuring performances of songs and poems being read by actors and public figures.

◥ www.shakespeares-sonnets.com.

  – Comprehensive site dedicated to the sonnets of Shakespeare containing contextual information and line by line analysis